C000174521

FROM
ABBERWICK
TO
YETLINGTON

THE PLACE-NAMES OF NORTH-EAST ENGLAND

IAN ROBINSON

Best Wishes,

Ian Robinson

June 2000

NORTHUMBERLAND TYNE AND WEAR
COUNTY DURHAM CLEVELAND

(C) Ian Robinson 1999

ISBN 0 9522480 8 5

Published by G P Electronic Services
87 Willowtree Avenue
Durham City DH1 1DZ
Tel: 0191 384 9707
Email: geoff1946@aol.com

Websites   www.gpelectronicservices.co.uk
             http://on-tyne.north-east.co.uk/History/tyneside-pp.asp

Modern photographs and front cover design (C) Geoff Phillips
Victorian sketches by I Wallace
Front cover photographs by Geoff Phillips: Background - Budle Bay, Bamburgh;
centre photograph - Durham Cathedral; top left - Penshaw Monument; top
right - The Angel of the North, Gateshead; bottom left - Middlesbrough
Transporter Bridge; bottom right - Bamburgh Castle.

ACKNOWLEDGMENTS

I would like to acknowledge my debt to the following learned volumes, on which
I have drawn extensively.

> Ekwall, E. *Concise Oxford Dictionary of English Place-Names* (OUP
> 1960)
> Reaney, P H. *The Origin of English Place-Names* (R&KP 1964)
> Cameron, K. *English Place-Names* (Batsford 1977)
> Jackson, C. *The Place-Names of Durham* (1916)
> Pevsner, N *The Buildings of England: County Durham* (1973)
> Room, A. *Concise Dictionary of Modern Place-Names* (OUP 1983)
> Rivet, A/Smith C. *The Place-Names of Roman Britain* (Batsford 1981)
> Mawer, Allen *The Place-Names of Northumberland and Durham* (1920)
> Beckensall, Steve *Durham Place-Names*
> Watson, G *Goodwife Hot and Other Places* (Sandhill 1970)

I would also like to thank the many listeners of BBC Radio Newcastle.

For Mam

CONTENTS

ABOUT THIS BOOK

We are all surrounded every day by ordinary words we see and use constantly, yet whose meanings are generally unknown to most of us. Place-names. This book is meant for the general reader who knows little or nothing about place-names but is curious to start finding out. So, although academics and expert toponymists (place-name people) may find this little volume interesting and enlightening, it is nevertheless intended for a wider audience of laymen - like me - whose curiosity has got the better of them, and who just 'want to know' a little bit more about the places and the names that surround them all day, every day.

That is why you will find no troublesome footnotes, no complicated abbreviations, and very few cross-references.

THE INTRODUCTION
If you are coming to the subject with only your curiosity and enthusiasm to keep you company, you should quite definitely read these introductory pages first - the Dictionary and Digest will make a lot more sense if you do!

The Introduction attempts to explain how places got their names by looking at the people who named them - where they came from and what language they spoke. It will also give you an idea of *when* places where named, and how they have changed over the centuries. It does this by explaining what I call 'the Six Ages of Place-Names' - the six main types of place-name grouped according to when the place was named and who was involved; to help you, you'll find examples of each of the six types of name. I have included a Time-Line, which attempts to put place-naming activity into an historical perspective.

And finally, in the section called 'How Place-Names Work', I put the theory into practise by looking at a selection of names and showing how they fit into the 'Six Ages'.

THE DICTIONARY
This is an alphabetical list of over 1400 place-names of North East England.
Usually, the meaning of each name is known, and is given in the Dictionary. Sometimes, though, experts are unsure of the precise meaning of a name, and this, too, is indicated in the Dictionary - you will find there many names which 'are probably..' or 'may be...' or 'seem to be...'. And you will find some which remain a complete mystery.

For composite place-names, you should look up the main part first. For GREAT

STAINTON, look up *STAINTON*; for WEST WHELPINGTON, look up *WHELPINGTON*. And remember that, for the purposes of this book, a 'place' is anywhere with a name. You will find in its pages reference not just to towns and villages, but also to farms, fields, rivers and hills.

THE DIGEST
Here you will find names grouped according to what they have in common - all names which mention animals, for example; or names which feature plants, or colours, or end in *-worth* or *-ley*.

There is also a list of those names I consider to be the region's oddest or most interesting. You might also like to look at the list of Place-Names Worth a Visit - places whose names feature elements like hills, rivers, buildings or other features which still exist and can still be seen.

And finally there's a look at the names of some of the area's 'lost' places - shrunken or completely abandoned villages which lie under its fields and hedgerows.

NOTE: NORTH EAST ENGLAND
Local government changes in 1974 and subsequently have played havoc with the traditional county boundaries used for centuries all over England. North East England has suffered particularly badly in this respect. Northumberland no longer extends southward to the Tyne; County Durham has lost territory here and gained it there; and two new counties - Cleveland and Tyne and Wear - have been created and, for most purposes, abolished as well.

In this book, North East England is all the land covered by the counties above, abolished or not. And, where counties are referred to in the book, they are the counties as established in 1974; that is, they include Tyne and Wear and Cleveland.

INTRODUCING THE PLACE-NAMES OF
NORTH EAST ENGLAND

To most of us nowadays, a place-name means simply the place to which it refers. *Darlington*, for example, means 'a moderately large market town in south-west County Durham'; *Yarm* is 'a market town on the south bank of the River Tees about 7 miles upstream'; *Cullercoats* is 'a seaside resort between Tynemouth and Whitley Bay'. But these definitions tell us nothing of the names themselves. Whose 'darling' is commemorated at Darlington? What was so special about the colour of the coats? And what exactly is a *yarm*?

Our problem is, of course, that most of England's place-names might as well be in a foreign language. Indeed, if you look in the Dictionary for the place-names mentioned above, you will see that they <u>are</u> in a foreign language. This is, in many ways, a pity. Most native Welsh speakers, for example, can understand the meaning of those mouth-fumbling Welsh place-names easily; and this is because, although the Welsh language has changed over the centuries, it has not changed very much.

English, however, has changed very much indeed since the days when local places were given their names. And, to make things more difficult, the language used in many of our place-names was not even the ancestor of Modern English; place-names of Celtic, Scandinavian, French and even Greek and Turkish origin can be found in North East England. All of this means that we need to search for the origins of names like *Wooler, Sherburn, Coulby* and *Consett*, which mean nothing to us at all.

Many of our local place-names do, in fact, wear their hearts on their sleeves. It seems to be obvious what they mean, we can safely take them at face value and not give them a second thought. *Blackhall*, for example, takes its name from the Black Hall caves which pierce the coastline hereabouts; *Hartburn* commemorates the many deer which once roamed by the stream here; *Seahouses* is honest-to-goodness 'houses by the sea' and *Rock* is - unsurprisingly - the name of a place where there was a particularly large boulder.

With some other place-names, a little imagination reveals all. *Seaham* is 'homestead by the sea' and - clever this one - *Beal* is 'bee hill'. Unfortunately, though, there aren't many place-names like this. The most we can expect is a tantalising titbit that we can understand, and a lot more that means nothing to our modern ears. There *are*, for example, cliffs - or at least steep banks - at *Egglescliffe, Coniscliffe* and *Horncliffe*, but what of *Eggles-*, *Conis-* and *Horn-* ? What sort of shield gave its name to *South Shields* and *Shieldfield*?

And with some place-names, an impenetrable fog descends, and no amount of informed guesswork or imagination can help. What are we to make of *Hett*, *Kyo*, *Ulgham* or - for Heaven's sake - *Wham*?

THE SIX AGES OF PLACE-NAMES

Most of the area's places have Old English names given during the Anglo-Saxon migration to Britain fourteen centuries ago. But many do not; some are, for example, Viking (from about the 8th century) or Norman (from 1066 onwards). And many are Modern names of the Industrial Age. To help lighten this place-name darkness and to unravel the jumble of types, dates and languages, I have always found it useful to think of The Six Ages of Place-Names

Although the Stone, Iron and Bronze Age peoples of these islands have left us many monuments and artifacts of their cultures, they left us virtually clueless about the languages they spoke; there are almost certainly no place-names at all which date from these times.

So the First Age of Place-Names is **CELTIC**.

The Celts, who spread across Europe from somewhere around Asia Minor, reached these shores about 450 BC. The language they spoke is now called Old British (or Old Welsh) and about fifty or so North East place-names include Old British words; *Consett*, *Kielder*, *Leven*, and *Cambois* are therefore - amongst others - the most ancient and venerable in this region, or any other. Old British names are indeed the oldest in England (*Britain* is a 'romanised' Celtic name), and we should respectfully bow our heads in recognition of their astonishing achievement in surviving two-and-a-half millennia, and at least four linguistic invasions.

Of course, descendants of the ancient Celtic people and their language still live on these islands, in Wales and Scotland. Popular history suggests that succeeding waves of migrants and invaders drove out the Celts westward but this is not so; look at the Dictionary entry for *Walworth*.

The Second Age came with the **ROMANS**.

The Romans invaded Britain about two thousand years ago, and easily overcame the peace-loving Celts. Within a hundred years or so, most of present-day England was under Roman control and - as elsewhere in the Empire - the native people

8

were 'romanised'; subject to Roman law and brought under the general influence of Roman culture and civilisation. The Roman presence was especially strong in this area, which was for many years the north-western edge of the Empire. As such, it needed to be effectively garrisoned and strongly defended. As well as the extensive remains of the remarkable Wall, over 70 miles long from coast to coast, present-day North East England is adorned with the ruins of a dozen or more Roman forts and supply stations, and laced with the tracks of many Roman roads.

Although no Roman place-names have survived intact into modern times, the influence of the names they used, and especially of the ruined Roman structures found and named by later settlers, was extensive. There is a section of the Digest devoted to the Romans and their place-names. The Romans left these shores gradually after about the 4th century.

The Third Age belongs to the **ANGLO-SAXONS**.

It is better to think of the Anglo-Saxon 'invasion' as a 'migration' which took place over many years, from about the 5th to the 8th centuries. Although the native Celts - abandoned by the Romans - are known to have attempted many stout defences of their territory against the newcomers, they were, in fact, virtually powerless against them. By the 8th century, the Anglo-Saxons occupied virtually all of present-day England (which is named after them) and, in doing so, permanently bequeathed us Old English, the ancestor of the language we are using now.

The new settlers quickly established themselves in their new land. Where necessary, land was cleared of trees and rocks - see the place-names from their word *leah*, 'clearing', in the Digest. They may then have built a *ham*, 'homestead', a *tun*, 'farmstead', or a *wic*, 'dairy farm'. If the farm was enclosed by a ditch or hedge, it was a *worth*. Sometimes their settlements were named after local features like hills, valleys, rivers and woods, or after the many wild animals and plants around them. The Digest gives more information about the kind of place-names handed down to us by the Anglo-Saxons. Their penetration locally was very deep; high ground and low, dry land and marshy, coast and hills, rivers, woods and valleys. This means that almost all of the place-names in Northumberland are of Anglo-Saxon origin, originating in Old English, and the proportion of such names is only slightly less in the rest of the area, as you will see from the Dictionary.

The Fourth Age is that of the **VIKINGS**.

The Vikings, from Norway and Denmark, began to raid our shores in the 7th century when, for example, the monastic settlements of Lindisfarne and Hartlepool were affected. Sporadic raids continued for a hundred years, although settlement in our area was quite sparse; the Vikings, for the most part, did not come ashore and stay here. It is likely that those who did simply settled in or near pre-existing Saxon villages - already numerous, as we have seen - so place-names in Old Norse, the Viking language, which are very common indeed south and west of this area, are comparatively rare hereabouts.

The commonest Viking place-name ending is -*by*, 'farm', and most of them mention the name of the settler concerned; *Aislaby*, *Killerby* and *Thornaby* are like this. There is more information in the Digest. Interestingly, the word *Viking* is derived from Old Norse *wic*, which originally meant 'harbour, haven'; Vikings were 'harbour people'. As the word passed to the Saxons, its meaning gradually changed to 'place for obtaining supplies' and then simply to 'dairy farm'. It can be found in local place-names as *wick*; *Butterwick*, *Elwick*, *Southwick*.

The Fifth Age is **NORMAN**.

Everybody knows that the Norman Conquest took place in 1066 (and all that). By this time, however, most places already had their names, which the new Norman overlords were quite happy to retain. Some new settlements were, however, established at this time, and (amongst others) *Beamish*, *Bellister*, *Causey* and *Pallion* all started life in Old French, the language of the conquerors.

French influence and fashion did, however, alter the 'style' of many pre-existing names. Baronial landowners' names stand on their own at *Guyzance* and *Darras* Hall, or were added at Hutton *Henry*, Coatham *Mundeville* and Morton *Palms*. And French difficulty in pronouncing certain English consonants changed the form of a few local names - both *Darlington* (which was Old English *Dearthingtun*) and *Durham* (which had been *Dunholm*) were affected in this way.

It is a remarkable tribute to the military thoroughness of the Conquest that so many local names originate - and have survived - in a language so utterly foreign to the Old and Middle English of the vanquished.

The Digest has a special section on Old French place-names.

The Sixth Age is **MODERN**.

Names given from about the 13th century onwards are all classed as 'modern'. If this seems rather drastic, you should remember that, by this time, most places already had their names, and in the last 700 years or so, place-naming activity has been sporadic.

The greatest modern place-name upsurge in North East England was caused by the rapid growth of industrial activity, especially coalmining. Although new pit villages often took the pre-existing name of an older neighbouring settlement - *Oakenshaw, Horden* - many adopted such a name by adding *Colliery,* or a similar word; Easington *Colliery*, Boldon *Colliery*, Esh *Winning*, Chevington *Drift*, Percy *Main*.

Others added *New* to an older name - *New* Brancepeth, *New* Herrington, *New* Coundon. And a large and colourful group of names reflect the patriotic fervour of the local magnate; *Toronto* and *Quebec* commemorate the 18th century Canadian Campaign; *Inkerman* and *Heights of Alma* do the same for the Crimea; *Blucher* and *Nelson* commemorate the struggle against Napoleon, whilst the conquest of America reverberates in *Philadelphia, California* and *New York*. There is a section on these, and many other, modern names in the Digest.

These, then, are the Six Ages from which all local place-names are descended. Although some names combine the Ages (*Cockerton* is a combination of Celtic *Cocker-* with Saxon *-ton*), almost all of them fall neatly into one group or another.

The time-line which follows this section should help put this sequence of invasions and place-naming languages into some sort of historical perspective.

THE SIX AGES TIME-LINE

Starting with the arrival of the Celts, this time-line shows, on the left-hand side, the waves of immigrations to, and invasions of, Britain over the last 2,500 years or so. The six corresponding ages of place-names are shown in the centre, with examples (where they exist). On the right are the dominant languages used by the new settlers.

Celtic immigration --
about 450 BC

> **1. CELTIC**
> *Tees, Wear, Keilder, Consett*
> and some others.

Old British
(Old Welsh)

Roman invasion ---
45 AD

> **2. ROMAN**

Latin

Roman evacuation - about 450 AD ---------------------------------

Anglo- Saxon immigration ---
from about 500 AD

> **3. ANGLO - SAXON**
> Almost all place-names ending in
> *-ham, -ton, -den, -worth,*
> *-cliffe, -ley, -chester, -well*
> *-wick, -field, -ford/forth,*
> and many others.

Old English

Viking immigation ---
from about 700 AD

> **4. VIKING**
> Almost all place-names ending in
> *-by, -thwaite*, and some others.

Old Scandinavian/
Old Norwegian

Norman conquest --
1066 AD

> **5. NORMAN FRENCH**
> *Bewley, Butterby, Causey,*
> and some others.

Old French/
Norman French

> **6. MODERN**
> *Percy Main, Toronto, Peterlee,*
> and many others.

Mostly
Modern English

HOW PLACE-NAMES WORK

You can see the Six Ages and the Time Line at work - as a sequence of invasions, migrations and changes of language - by looking at a few of the Dictionary's entries under just one letter.....P.

It surprises many newcomers to place-names that there are so many of Welsh origin in so 'English' an area as this. The ancient Celts, though, were the 'original' inhabitants of this area (apart from the prehistoric people who have left us their standing stones and stone circles to admire and wonder at). The Celts had, after all, been living here for 500 years when Hadrian had his Wall built.

Plenmeller, which even sounds vaguely unEnglish, is a Celtic name of the First Age, and is almost certainly well over two thousand years old. Even so, it equates exactly to Modern Welsh *blaen-moelfre*, 'bare hilltop'. In so doing, it gives us a glimpse of the area's geographical history. Nowadays, virtually all the local hilltops are 'bare', but in Celtic times - and for centuries afterwards - the area was densely forested, making a 'bare hilltop' worth remarking upon.

Penshaw (like *Painshaw*) seems to be a First Age name. Even without its monument, Penshaw Hill would be a striking geographical feature; local folklore links it to the legend of the Lambton Worm, whilst local people still use the hill for traditional Easter egg-rolling, an activity known to originate in ancient, pagan rituals.

The name itself may well be a combination of two Celtic words meaning 'at the top of the rocks' - *pen-cerr*. The meaning seems appropriate, and the name's survival through waves of later settlers - and their languages - points to its sanctity.

Pont is also thought to be a First Age name. It is one of many local river-names which date back to the area's Celtic aborigines and, in this case, their word for 'valley'.

Unusually, the same name is found again further south as part of *Pontop*. Like a few other local names, this one is tautological - it says the same thing twice. As we have seen, the *pont* part of the name is First Age - Celtic 'valley'. Later Anglo-Saxon settlers adopted the name but did not, of course, know what it meant; they spoke a completely different language. To give the name some meaning to themselves, they added their own word for 'valley' - *hop* (which you will also find in *Westerhope* and *Cassop*). The name thus became pont-hop, 'valley valley'!

Pons Aelius - 'the bridge of Aelius' - brings us into the Second Age of Place-

Names. It is the name the Romans gave their settlement on the north bank of the Tyne. Interestingly, the fort here was not just geographically close to the Wall - it was linguistically close to it, as well; *Aelius* was the the family name of the Emperor Hadrian, who ordered the Wall's construction and gave it his 'proper' name.

No Second Age - Roman - names survived intact into modern times, but *Piercebridge* serves to illustrate what happened to many of them. The Romans built a substantial fort here, as well as an imposing bridge over the Tees; the remains of both can still be seen. They may have called their settlement *Morbium*. After they left, however, the fort was abandoned to decay and ruin until Anglo-Saxon settlers came upon it about two centuries later.

Sensibly, they made use of the stone to build themselves a new village here, and naturally they gave it an Old English (Third Age) name; 'bridge by the osier willows' - *Piercebridge*. The original Latin name would long since have been forgotten and, in any case, the Saxons would not have known what it meant. Indeed, we still do not know what *Morbium* meant.

So we are now into the Third Age of local place-names; the Anglo-Saxon age.

Many of the Anglo-Saxon personal names you will find in the Dictionary have disappeared from our language altogether, and seem utterly foreign to modern ears. *Esi*, who settled at *Easington*, is one. *Paelli* is another. We know that a Saxon settler called Paelli built a farmstead and called it *Paelli-tun*; Pelton. He also seems to have laid claim to the nearby prehistoric burial-mound or barrow (*hlaw* in Old English) calling it *Paelli-hlaw*; Pelaw. It is rare for the same person to be commemorated in adjacent place-names like this; Paelli must have been quite important.

With *Plawsworth*, we are still with our Anglo-Saxon settlers of the 5th - 8th centuries. This name seems to give the lie to an image of po-faced aggressive and humourless men and women sitting around flickering fires in the rain looking miserable; it means 'the enclosure where games were played'. Unfortunately, we do not know what the games were.

Preston is a Third Age name, too, and is common throughout England. It means 'priest's farmstead'. *Preston Grange* casts light on mediaeval farming practise; a *grange* - from an Old French word - was an outlying farm directly tied to, and managed by, a much larger, landowner's estate farm.

Preston le Skerne introduces a Viking, Fourth Age, element. The name of this little river is Old English *scir*, 'bright, clear', but spelt and pronounced in a Viking way - the Saxon pronunciation is found in <u>Sherburn</u>.

In place-name terms, *Pallion* is comparatively recent; the first known written form of the name was *le Pavylion* in 1328. The name looks French, and indeed it is; the Normans, under William the Conqueror, had brought their language over to Britain with the Conquest of 1066, and quite a few local places were given names in Old French, as it is known now. These are our Fifth Age names.

The 14th century meaning of *pavylion* was very close to the meaning of our modern word 'pavilion'; a structure built for a special purpose - probably recreational - and 'belonging' to another building. Unfortunately, we will probably never know the purpose of the pavilion that was built here, though it may well have been a sort of retreat or rest home for the monks of nearby Wearmouth and Jarrow.

Plashetts, too, is a Fifth Age name, and serves as a reminder of what could happen to a French name when subjected to the alien sound-system of Middle English!

We enter the Sixth Age with *Port Clarence*, a name which marks the dawn of the modern industrial age which did so much to shape the land and people of this area. The Tees and Weardale Railway Company needed better transshipment facilities than existed at its Stockton terminus, and so extended its line nearer the sea in 1827. The industrial and residential settlement which developed was named after the Duke of Clarence who, three years later, became King William IV.

Peterlee brings us right into the 20th century. The town is a result of the post-war policy of rehousing miners and their families away from traditional colliery terraces into new 'garden city' avenues. It was built on a 'greenfield' site, and was named - cleverly and innovatively - in honour of Peter Lee, a local miners' union leader who died in 1935.

The letter P in the Dictionary takes us up other place-name avenues and even cul-de-sacs. *Pennines*, for example, is a great and valuable rarity - a pure place-name invention, concocted in the 18th century by a zealous local historian to *sound* First Age. And it does.

With *Pity Me* and *Page Bank* we are in a separate and unique category. No-one seems to know what these names mean and, frustratingly, it seems that no-one ever will.

I hope that this brief scan of just a few names shows that, in satisfying our idle curiosity about the meaning of place-names, we also learn - almost accidentally - about many other aspects of our history, geography, languages and the society that produced us.

AND....

When we learn about places and the meanings of their names, we almost accidentally learn much else about the day-to-day lives of our ancestors. We find out, for example, about the crops they grew - wheat at *Wheatley Hill*, apples at *Eppleton* and *Apperley,* rye at *Ryton* and *Ryle* - and about the plants that grew all around them, and which they harvested - willows at *Piercebridge*, hazelnuts at *Hesleden* (and *Hesledon* and *Hazlerigg*), briars at *Brierton,* cranberries at *Barmoor* and hay at *Aydon.*

We learn about the animals they reared - cattle at *Coundon, Stella* and *Burdon,* pigs at *Swinhope* and *Swinburn,* horses at *Stotfold* and *Horsley* and even bees at *Beal* and *Bickerton*; the animals that lived in the encircling woods and hills - bison at *Urpeth* and *Urlay Nook,* wolves at *Ushaw, Wooden* and *Wooley,* wildcats at *Catton, Catcleugh* and *Cassop,* deer at *Hart, Hendon, Hartburn, Hartley* and *Harton* - and of how they caught them at *Kepier* and *Slingley.* We even know of their pests at *Hamsterley* (not hamsters), *Embleton* and *Migley.*

We learn how comparatively peacefully different nationalities lived amongst each other - Scots at *Shotton* and *Shotley,* Irish at *Ireshopeburn,* the ancient Celts (Welsh) at *Wallish Walls* and *Walworth,* Angles (English) at *Ingleton* and *Ingleby,* Norsemen at *Normanby* and even a Belgian at *Flemingfield.*

We find a hint of our ancestors' mythic and religious beliefs at *Harle, Harrowgate* and *Shincliffe,* and of their occupations at *Harperley, Hunterley, Preston, Sacriston, Coulby, Lesbury, Wardley* and *Nunstainton.*

And we realise how very poor roads were and that bridges were almost non-existent; this is why fords across rivers were of vital importance, and why settlements invariably developed around them - *Gosforth, Allensford, Gainsford, Startforth.* And at *Catchgate* we learn how mediaeval roads were paid for and maintained.

Farms, hamlets, villages and towns have been founded and developed continuously since prehistoric times, and this is reflected in the enormous variety of the names we have chosen to give them over the centuries. And the process is, of course, still going on. New names will be given to new settlements, and new dictionaries like this one will need to include them.

For me, finding out about the real meaning of place-names has been a years-long voyage of surprise, discovery and pleasure. This introduction - indeed, this book - is my attempt to pass on this pleasure to you.

Winlaton, Tyne and Wear
Old English, meaning 'Winelac's farmstead'

Abberwick, near Alnwick, Northumberland

ABBERWICK
Old English 'Aluburg's dairy farm'. *Aluburg* is a woman's name.
ACKLAM
Old English 'at the oak clearings'.
ACKLINGTON
Old English 'farmstead of Eadlac's people'.
ACOMB
Old English *acum*, 'at the oak trees'. There are at least two places with this name, including EAST ACOMB.
ACTON
Old English 'Acca's farmstead'.
ADDERSTONE
Old English 'Eadred's farmstead'.
AIKENSHAW
Old English 'oak wood' - the same as *Oakenshaw*, below.
AISLABY
Old Norse 'Aslakr's village (or homestead)'. There are two.
AKELD
Old English *ac-helde*, 'oak slope'.

ALDEN (ALDIN) GRANGE

First appears in the charters of Finchale Priory as *Aldingrig*, so no 'grange' is involved here. The name, from Old English, means 'Ealda's ridge'.

ALDWORTH

Old English 'old farmstead enclosure'.

ALLEN *(River)*

Like many local river and hill names, *Allen* is of ancient Celtic origin, and almost certainly means 'holy one' or 'mighty one'. The river's valley is ALLENDALE, wherein lies ALLENDALE TOWN. The river rises at ALLENHEADS. See also *Aln*, *Alwin* below.

ALLENSFORD

Old English 'Aella's ford' (across the Derwent).

ALLERDEAN

Old English 'alder valley' or 'Aelfhere's valley'. Nearby is WEST ALLERDEAN.

ALLERWASH

Old English 'alder swamp'. In Staffordshire, the same name appears as *Alrewas*.

ALN *(River)*

Said to be derived from the same Celtic root-word as *Allen*, above. The river has given its name to ALNHAM ('homestead by the Aln', and pronounced *alnm*), ALNWICK ('dairy farm by the Aln', pronounced *annick*) and ALNMOUTH (properly pronounced *almth*).

Alnmouth, Northumberland

ALWIN *(River)*

Said to derive from the same Celtic root-word as *Allen* and *Aln*, above. By the river is ALWINTON.

AMBLE

First recorded as *Ambell* in 1204; this is Old English 'Anna's headland'. The second part of this name is equivalent to Modern English 'bill', as in Portland *Bill.*

AMERSTON

Old English 'Amund's farmstead'.

ANCROFT

Old English 'lonely croft'.

ANGERTON

Old English 'farmstead with grazing land'.

ANGRYHAUGH

Old English 'water-meadow used for grazing'. The first, 'angry', part of this name is also found in *Angerton*, above, and *Ingram*, below.

ANICK

May be Old English 'Egelwin's farm'. This may be the same Egelwin who was Bishop of Durham in the 11th century.

ANNFIELD PLAIN

Early forms of *Annfield* are rare; the name probably means simply 'Ann's field' - *Ann* was a man's name in Saxon times. The addition of *Plain* is recent, and refers to the inclined plane sited nearby, and built to convey coal tubs up an otherwise unmanageable slope.

ANNITSFORD

Seems to be Old English 'ford at the end of a steep path'.

APPERLEY

Old English 'apple-tree clearing'.

ARBEIA

See *SHIELDS*, below, and *The Romans and Place-Names* in the Digest.

ARCHDEACON NEWTON

This rather stately name is thought to have arisen when, in mediaeval times, the 'new farmstead' here was held by lease under the Archdeacon of Durham.

ASHINGTON

Old English *aescen-denu*, 'ash-tree valley'.

AUCKLAND

The derivation of this name is uncertain. The earliest recorded versions of the name appear as *Alclit, Alclat, Alcleat,* and *Aclet.* Some authorities suppose that the name was 'transferred' from *Alcluith*, the eighth-century name Bede recorded for the Clyde Valley (in Scotland). This is possible: at the time *Clyde* - an old Celtic word - meant simply 'river'. Auckland may thus mean '(by the) river valley'.

BISHOP AUCKLAND *Bishop* was added to the name in the twelfth century, when the Prince Bishops decided to make their permanent residence at Auckland Palace.

ST ANDREW AUCKLAND A separate parish in the south-eastern corner of Auckland. Local people call the settlement *SOUTH CHURCH*.

ST HELEN (ST HELENS) AUCKLAND This part of Auckland surrounds the 13th century church of St Helen.

WEST AUCKLAND takes its name from its position - actually south-west of Auckland proper.

AXWELL PARK

First appears as *Aksheles* as late as the fourteenth century. It is descended from Old Norse *ack* (oak) and *schele* (hut, shelter, shielings), and means the 'shelter by the oak trees' *Park* refers to the parkland laid out around the country house here in 1758.

AYCLIFFE

The different settlements hereabouts may have different meanings.

GREAT AYCLIFFE is the 'proper' name of old Aycliffe village, and may go back to Saxon *ac leah*, 'clearing in the oak trees'.

NEWTON AYCLIFFE is a modern place with a modern 'Newton' added to the name of the old village nearby.

SCHOOL AYCLIFFE The 'Aycliffe' here may be Old English *ac-clif*, 'steep bank by the oak trees'. The presence of *School* is unusual and misleading. It refers to someone called *Scula*, who was granted land here by the Church in the tenth century.

AYDON, near Corbridge

From Old English *heg-denu*, 'hay valley'.

AYDON, near Alnwick

Old English *heg-dun*, 'hay hill'.

AYKLEY HEADS

The name may be Old English 'clearing amongst the oaks (*Aykley*) on the hilltop'.

AYLE (BURN)

Said to be derived from the same ancient Celtic word as *Allen*, *Aln* and *Alwin* above.

BACKWORTH

Old English 'Bacca's farmstead enclosure'.

BAGRAW

Seems to be Old and Middle English 'row (of huts) where hawkers live', although it has also been suggested that the name refers to a 'beggarly row'.

BALDER *(River)*

May - like many river names - be of Celtic origin, meaning 'peak stream'. Another theory, though, suggests that *BALDERSDALE* - the valley through which it flows

- is the original name, from Old Norse 'Baldhere's valley', and that the river was named after the valley (rather than the other way round).

BAMBURGH
Old English 'Bebbe's fortified place'. Bebbe was the queen of Aethelfrith, 7th century king of Northumbria.

BARDON MILL
Middle English 'mill near Bardon'. BARDON is Old English 'barrow hill'; a barrow is a prehistoric burial mound.

BARLOW
First appears in 1185 as *Berley*, and means 'the barley clearing'.

BARMOOR
Old English 'cranberry moor'.

BARMSTON
Old English 'Beornmund's (or perhaps Beorn's) farmstead'.

BARMPTON
Old English 'Beornmund's farmstead'. *Beorn* and *Beornmund* were fairly common forenames in Saxon times; the modern Scandinavian equivalent is *Björn*.

BARNARD CASTLE
The town grew up around, and takes its name from, the castle built here on a rocky outcrop above the River Tees by Bernard Balliol in the early 12th century; the ruins of the castle can, of course, still be seen.

BARNINGHAM
Old English 'homestead of Beorn's people'.

BARRASFORD
Old English 'ford by a grove'.

BAVINGTON
Old English 'farmstead of Babba's people'.

BEADNELL
Old English 'Beda's little nook'. Another Beda gave his name to *Bedburn*; see below.

BEAL
Old English *beo-hyll*, 'bee hill'.

BEAMISH
'Of Norman French origin. It appears in 1288 as *Bewmys*, and means 'beautiful mansion', the same as the French place-name *Beaumetz*. Nearby, at a once important crossing point of the small stream, is the hamlet of *BEAMISH BURN*.

BEANLEY
Old English 'clearing where beans were grown'.

BEARL
Old English 'barley hill'.

BEARPARK
No bears or parks are involved here. A place of rest and solitude for his monks

was founded here in about 1250 by Prior Bartram of Durham; he called it *Beaurepaire*, a French name meaning 'beautiful retreat'. and the modern name is a corruption of this. *Belper*, in Derbyshire, is derived in the same way and *Beaurepaire* survives, uncorrupted, as the name of another village in Hampshire.

BEAUFRONT (CASTLE)
Of Norman French origin; 'beautiful brow (of a hill)'.

BEBSIDE
May be Old English 'Bibba's bit of land'.

BEDBURN
Old English 'Beda's stream'. A different Beda gave his name to *Beadnell,* above.

BEDLINGTON
Old English 'farmstead of Bedla's people'. Nearby is the more recent settlement of BEDLINGTON STATION.

BELASIS and BELLASIS
First appear at the turn of the 14th century, and come from Old French *bel assize*, 'beautiful site'.

BELFORD
Although this name may be Old English 'Bela's ford', its precise origins are unknown.

BELLINGHAM
Old English 'homestead of the hill-dwellers'. The name is pronounced *belinjm*.

BELLISTER
From Norman French *bel-estre*, 'fine place'.

BELMONT
This name comes to us from Old French, and means 'beautiful hill'.

BELSAY
Old English 'Bill's ridge'.

BELSHILL
Probably Old English 'shelter on the hill'.

BELTINGHAM
Seems to be Old English 'homestead of Belthor's people'. It is pronounced *beltinjm*.

BENFIELDSIDE
A fairly late Old English name meaning 'slope with a bean-field (or a field of bentgrass)'.

BENRIDGE
Old English 'bean ridge'.

BENTON
Old English 'farmstead where bent-grass (or, perhaps, beans) grew'. *LONG-* was added as a description of the Saxon settlement, and to distinguish it from nearby LITTLE BENTON.

BENWELL
No well is involved here. The name started life in Old English as *bionnan walle*, 'inside the wall'. The settlement lies between Hadrian's Wall and the River Tyne.
BERRINGTON
Old English 'hill with a fortification'.
BERWICK UPON TWEED
Old English 'corn farm'. For *Tweed*, see below.
BEWICK
Old English 'bee farm'. Nearby is the site of the original settlement, now OLD BEWICK, as well as BEWICK BRIDGE.
BEWLEY
A 14th century Old French name meaning 'beautiful place', like *Beaulieu* in Hampshire. The Cleveland village is really *NEWTON BEWLEY*, presumably so-called because the original settlement was replaced.

> COWPEN BEWLEY No cows or pens here. The first element is from a Middle English word meaning (hen) coops. Indeed, local people pronounce the name *coopn*.

BICKERTON
Old English 'farmstead of the bee-keeper'.
BIDDICK
From Old English *bi dic*, 'beside the ditch'. Until recently, this mining village was known by some local people as *Butney*, a corruption of *Botany* (Bay), presumably because working conditions in the pit were so awful.
BIDDLESTONE
Old English 'valley with a dwelling in it'. The first part of this name is related to *Budle* and New*bottle*.
BILDERSHAW
Seems to be Old English 'Baldhere's wood'.
BILLINGHAM
Appears, spelt exactly as now, in 1050, and means 'the homestead (*ham*) of Bill's people (*Billingas*)'.
BILLY MILL
was 'Billing's mill' in 1320.
'BILLY ROW
Billy is Old English 'Billa's clearing'. Although *Row* was sometimes used locally to mean 'open country', here it probably means a row of huts. Another Billa settled at *Bilton*, below.
BILTON
Old English 'Billa's farmstead'.
BINCHESTER
The second part of the name is from the common Old English *ceastre*, 'a Roman

fort', as in *Lanchester, Ebchester* and *Chester-le-Street*. The first part, though, is uncertain; it may come from a word *binn*, 'animal shelter, manger' - perhaps the old fort was used for this purpose. Alternatively, it could be a corruption of the first part of the Latin name for the fort, which was *VINOVIA*. The meaning of this name is itself unknown.

BINGFIELD
Old English 'Bynna's pastureland'.

BIRKENSIDE
Middle English 'birch-covered slope'.

BIRTLEY
Old English *beorhte leah*, 'bright clearing'.

BISHOPTON
First occurs in the 12th century as *Biscoptun*, and means 'the farmstead (or manor) of the Bishop (of Durham)'. The *motte*, or mound, on which the castle stood is still visible here.

BITCHBURN, NORTH
Takes its name from the Beechburn Beck, which passes by here. Early versions of this name make interpretation difficult. It may mean either 'beech stream' or 'Bicca's stream'. Oddly, there is no South, East or West Bitchburn.

BITCHFIELD
Old English 'pastureland amongst beech-trees'.

BLACKHALL
This 20th century colliery settlement takes its name from the Black Hall caves which undermine the cliffs here. Local usage divides the settlement in two; *BLACKHALL COLLIERY* and *BLACKHALL ROCKS*, a later development to the south. The 'rocks' are the boulders and stacks which line the adjacent coast.

BLACKHILL
Unsurprisingly, Old English 'black hill'.

BLACK MIDDENS and BLACK MIDDINGS
Both locations take their names from Old Norse *middyng*, 'dungheap, cesspit', still used in the North East. The coastal and under-river rocks are a formidable and hated danger to shipping; it is difficult to see why inland Black Middings was so-named - perhaps it was simply an unusually unpleasant spot to eke out a living.

BLACKWELL
Middle English 'the black spring'.

BLAGDON
Old English 'black valley'.

BLAKELAW
Old Norse 'black hill'.

BLANCHLAND
This unusual and sonorous name was transferred from *Blanche-Launde* in

Normandy. It is Old French 'white launde'. *Launde* is Norman French 'glade', and is related to Modern English 'lawn'.

BLAYDON

Early versions of this name are confusing, though it is probably Old English 'black hill' (*blar dun*).

BLEAKLAW

Old English 'black hill'.

BLENKINSOPP

Old English 'Blenkin's valley'. *Blenkin* is a Celtic name meaning 'hill-dweller'.

BLUCHER

A colliery village named by the coal-owner in honour of General Blucher, Wellington's ally at the Battle of Waterloo in 1815. Other names depicting high points of British imperial history are in the *Modern Names* part of the Digest.

BLYTH *(River)*

This is the same word for 'merry, happy' still found in Modern English. The town of BLYTH - which was *Blythmouth* in the 13th century - obviously takes its name from the river.

BOCKENFIELD

Old English 'beech field'.

BOLAM

There is considerable disagreement about the origin of this name. The two main contenders are Old English 'Bol's homestead (*ham*)' or - in the same language - '(the place at) the tree trunks' (*bolum*).

BOLDON

Old English 'hill with a homestead'. There are three Boldons; EAST and WEST BOLDON, and nearby BOLDON COLLIERY.

BOLDRON

Old Norse 'cleared space for a bull'.

BOLLIHOPE

Early forms of the name suggest a meaning like 'Bol's valley' (see *Bolam*, above).

BOLTON

Old English 'farmstead with a cottage'.

BOOSBECK

I can find no explanation for this sonorous name.

BOTHAL

Old English 'Bota's little nook'.

BOULBY

Probably Old Norse 'Bola's farm'.

BOULMER

Middle English 'bullock lake'. The name is pronounced *boomer*.

BOURNMOOR

Seems to be Middle English 'stream on a moor'. Local people pronounce the first element *burn*.

BOWBURN
May be Old English 'bow-shaped stream'.

BOWES
First recorded in the 12th century as *Bogas* and *Bogis*. It is probably derived from Old English *boga* and means 'arched bridges'. The Roman fort here was called *LAVATRIS*, which may have been a latinization of an Old Celtic word for 'river-bed'.

BOWSDEN
Old English 'hill with a dwelling'.

BRADBURY
There are at least two possible explanations for the name. The terminal -*bury* is from Old English *burg*, 'fortified place'; the first element may mean 'broad, wide', or 'made with boards, planks'.

BRADFORD
Old English 'wide (broad) ford'.

BRADLEY
From Old English *brad-leah*, 'broad (wide) clearing'. The name is really HIGH BRADLEY, and the farm here overlooks the single-terrace settlement of BRADLEY COTTAGES.

BRAFFERTON
Old English *brad* 'wide' and *ford* 'ford' and *tun* 'farmstead'; 'the farmstead by the wide ford' (across the River Skerne).

BRAINSHAUGH
May be Old English 'water-meadow with a burial mound'.

BRANCEPETH
Appears as *Brentespethe* in 1085 and *Brandespethe* in 1155. The second element is a local dialectal form of 'path, road'. The first part is trickier. It may refer either to someone called Brant, or to nearby Brandon. Thus we have either 'Brant's path', or 'the path to Brandon'.

> Local folklore explains the name as 'brawn's path', and links it to the legend of The Brawn of Brancepeth, a 'horride brawne' or wild boar killed by one Hodge of Ferry.

About 2m away is the colliery village of NEW BRANCEPETH.

BRANDON
Old English *brom-dun*, 'broom hill'.

BRANTON
Old English 'farmstead amongst the broom'.

BRANXTON
Old English 'Branoc's farmstead'.

BRASSIDE
May be Old English 'hillside'.

BREAMISH *(River)*
Like many river-names, this is of ancient Celtic origin; it is thought to mean 'roaring'.

BRECKON HILL
Old English 'bracken hill'.

BREMENIUM
See *ROCHESTER*, below, and *The Romans and Place-Names* in the Digest.

BRENKLEY
Old Norse 'Brynca's hill'.

BRIERTON
Old English 'the farmstead where briars (or thorns) grew'.

BRIGNALL
May be Old English 'Bryni's corner of land'.

BRINKBURN
Old English 'Brynca's stream'.

BROCOLITIA
See *CARRAW*, below, and *The Romans and Place-Names* in the Digest.

BROOM
Although claims have been made that this name is a corruption of *Browney*, the stream by which the village stands, it more probably comes from Old English *brom*, 'broom' (the plant); thus 'the place where broom grows'. Local usage adds *PARK* to this name.

BROOMHAUGH
Old English 'broom-covered water-meadow'.

BROOMHILL
Old Norse 'broom hill'.

BROOMHOPE
Old English 'broom valley'.

BROOMLEY
Old English 'clearing amongst broom (or brambles)'.

BROTHERWICK
Old English 'Brodor's dairy farm'. *Brodor* is related to Modern English *brother*, and may here be an affectionate nickname; 'colleague, brother-in-arms'.

BROTTON
Recorded as *Broctune* in Domesday Book. It is Old English 'farmstead on a brook'.

BROWNEY *(River)*
This name started life as Old English *brune*, 'the brown one'. The *-ey* at the end was added later, and may be Old English *ea*, 'river'. The village of BROWNEY is a colliery settlement by the river.

BROWNIESIDE
Old English 'on the side of the brown hill'.

BROXFIELD
Old English 'pastureland on a brook'.
BRUNTON
Old English 'farmstead by the burn (brook)'. There are at least five Bruntons, including EAST, WEST, NORTH and BRUNTON BRIDGE.
BRUSSELTON
There are no early forms of the name, though it may mean 'Beorht's farmstead'.
BUCKTON
Seems to be Old English 'Bucca's farmstead', although it has also been suggested that the land here was transferable by deed, or 'book'; that this is 'book-land'.
BUDLE
Old English 'dwelling'. The name is related to the second part of Wal*bottle* and New*bottle*.
BULBECK COMMON
Preserves the name of the Norman French family from Bolbec on the Seine, who held the land.
BURDON
Early Old English forms of the name suggest 'valley with a byre (or dwelling)' - *byr-denu*.
BURDON, GREAT
Comes from Old English *burg-dun*, 'hill with a fortification'. *GREAT* is a common place-name prefix, obviously used to differentiate between adjacent large and small places with the same name. *Little Burdon* has, here, disappeared, although the farmstead of *Old Burdon* lies nearby.
BURGHAM
Old English 'homestead by the fortification'.
BURNHOPE
Old English 'stream valley'.
BURNOPFIELD
Related to *Burnhope*, above; it is Old English 'open land by the valley stream'.
BURNTSHIEL
Old English 'burnt hut'.
BURRADON
Old English 'hill with a fortification'.
BUSTON
Old English 'Buttel's hill'. The settlement is divided into HIGH and LOW BUSTON.
BUTELAND
Old English 'Bota's land'.
BUTSFIELD
The second element here is Old English *feld* 'open country, land free from woods,

outlying enclosure'. The meaning of the first element is uncertain; it could be a personal name like *Bot* or *Bota*; or it could refer to a *butte*, a small, irregular-shaped piece of land. There are two settlements here: EAST and WEST BUTSFIELD.

BUTTERBY
Derived from Old French *beautroue*, 'beautiful find'.

BUTTERKNOWLE
Seems to be Old English 'hill where butter is made', or possibly 'fruitful, productive hill'.

BUTTERLAW
Old English 'butter-productive hill'.

BUTTERWICK
Recorded in 1131 in almost exactly this form, the name means 'butter farm, dairy farm'.

BYERMOOR
Old English 'Beaghere's moor'.

BYERS GREEN
A comparatively late name, first recorded in 1345 as *Bires*. It is probably the exact equivalent of modern 'byres', and means '(the green by the) cowsheds'.

BYKER
Recorded as *Bikere* in 1196 and already *Byker* by 1212. It seems to be Old Norse *by-kiarr*, 'the village marsh'.

BYSHOTTLES
The defunct alternative Old English name for Brandon, near Durham; it may mean either 'the town latrines' or 'the town lock-up'.

BYWELL
Old English *byge-wella*, 'wellspring in a bend'. The bend is in the River Tyne, for which see below.

CAISTRON
Old English 'thorntree by a marsh'.

CALIFORNIA
Obviously the name of an American state, it may have arisen here as an ironic field-name, given by a farmer to a particularly productive - or perhaps distant - field.

CALLALY
Old English 'clearing for calves'.

CALLERTON
Old English 'hill where calves grazed'. Nearby is BLACK CALLERTON, presumably because of the colour of the soil, and HIGH CALLERTON.

CAMBO
This unusual name derives from Old English *camb-hoh*, 'hillspur (*hoh*) with a comb (or crest)'.

CAMBOIS
This is an ancient British name, identical with Gaelic *camus*, and pronounced in the same way. It means 'bay'. Later Saxon settlers were unaware of this, and added their own word *Bay* to the name of the geographical feature; 'Bay Bay'.

CAPHEATON
See *HEATON*, below.

CARGO FLEET
'Cold shelters by a stream'. This modern-sounding name is, in fact, very ancient. It was first recorded in the 13th century as *Caldecotes*, 'cold huts' (or perhaps 'huts used for shelter in the cold'). Precisely how this became *Cargo* is something of a mystery, as is the timing of the addition of Old English *fleot*, 'stream' (which is, of course, the origin of London's River *Fleet* and *Fleet* Street).

CARHAM
Old English 'at the rocks'.

CARLBURY
This name seems to be Old English *Ceorlaburg,* but altered to something like *Carlesburi* by later Scandinavian (Viking) settlers. *Burg/buri* is 'fortified place'; *Ceorla/carls* refers either to 'free peasants', or to a settler called Carl.

CARLIN (CARLING) HOW
The first word is from Old Norse *kerling*, 'old woman, hag', and the second is Old Norse for 'hill' - 'the hill of the old woman'. Interestingly, this may well have been a hill where witches were thought to gather.

CARLTON
May be the Viking version of Old English *Ceorletun*. The name means 'the farmstead of the free peasants' or 'of Carl'.

CARRAW
Probably derived from an ancient Celtic word meaning 'rocks'. CARRAWBURGH is Old English 'fortification near Carraw', and refers to the site of a Roman fort. When it was occupied, the fort was called *BROCOLITIA* by the Romans. Several explanations have been given for this name: 'infested with badgers'; 'full of pointed rocks'; or 'covered with heather'.

CARRSHIELD
Old English 'shelter at the marsh' or 'on a rocky slope'.

CARRVILLE
I can find no record of the Carr after whom this suburb is named.

CARTERWAY HEADS
Middle English 'hilltop with a road used by carts'.

CARTINGTON
Old English 'hill of Certa's people'.

CASSOP
There seem to be two possible meanings here. The second element is Old English

hop, 'valley'. The first is either the Saxon personal name *Casa* ('Casa's valley'), or Old English *cattes*, 'wildcat' (thus 'valley of wildcats').

There are two settlements here. The original, now called OLD CASSOP, lies in the valley; the more recent village, which developed around the colliery, sits on the ridge above.

CASTLE EDEN
There are two quite contrary explanations for the name of the Eden burn, which flows through the village. One authority gives it as Old English *Godene*, 'God's valley' (*God* here is a personal name, perhaps meaning 'good'). Another suggests that, like many river names, Eden is descended from an ancient British - Celtic - word, in this case meaning 'gushing'. The village developed around the castle, which was built between 1758 and 1780.

CASTLESIDE
Seems to be Middle English 'hillside by a castle'. The 'castle' could be the extensive earthworks at nearby Rowley.

CATCHBURN
Old English 'Caecca's stream'.

CATCHGATE
In mediaeval times, upkeep of roads and tracks was paid for by the levying of tolls on road users, payable at tollgates - or tollbars - placed at strategic points. To avoid the toll, merchants and other travellers would try to use side-roads or back lanes; a 'catchgate' was a tollhouse erected on such a lane to 'catch' them.

CATCLEUGH
Old English 'clough (ravine) of wildcats'. The hill of CATCLEUGH SHIN uses a transferred lowland Scots word for 'steep slope'.

CATTON
Old English 'wildcat valley'.

CAUSEY
Originated as Old French *caucie*, 'embankment, raised way'. In Modern English, popular etymology has changed this word - quite incorrectly - to *causeway*.

CAWFIELDS
Seems to be late Old English 'Cawa's pasturelands'.

CAWLEDGE
Late Old English 'Cawa's slow-moving stream'. The second part of this name - *ledge* - survives in modern Northumbrian dialect as *letch*, 'slow moving stream'.

CHARLTON
See *Carlton*, above.

CHATHILL
Old English 'Ceotta's hill'.

CHATTON
Old English 'Ceatta's farmstead'.

CHEESEBURN

There is some disagreement about the derivation of this name. It may be descended from two Old English words for 'cheese' and 'fortification', although the precise meaning of this combination of ideas is, perhaps thankfully, unknown. Alternatively, it has been suggested that its meaning is 'gravelly stream'.

CHESTERHOLM

Old English 'Roman fort' with Old Norse 'island'; 'island by a Roman fort'. The Romans called their fort here *VINDOLANDA*, meaning perhaps 'bright moor' or 'fair moor'.

CHESTER LE STREET

It is best to start with the Roman name for their fort here - *CONCANIS*. The meaning of this name is uncertain, although it is thought to be descended from an ancient pre-Roman Celtic root-word denoting 'horse-people' (literally or metaphorically). Later Saxon settlers used the Roman name, but added *ceastre* - their word for a Roman fort - to it. Thus it was as *Cunceceastre* that the name was first recorded in 1050. Quite soon, the name was simply *Ceastre* - 'Chester', which for local people suffices to this day.

However, under Norman French influence, distinction was added with *en le Street* - 'in the Street' (over time, the *en* was dropped). *Street* was used from Saxon times to the Middle Ages to denote a Roman road. Thus we arrive at 'The Roman fort by the Roman road'.

Interestingly, the settlement's ancient Roman citizens may still be haunting the town; the stream which flows through its centre is called the *Cong Burn* - a memory of *Concanis*? - and the place where the Roman road crosses it is known as the *Point* - could we have Latin *pont* ('bridge') here?

Chester-le-Street. 1888.

CHESTER MOOR
Middle English 'moor near a Roman fort' or 'beside Chester le Street'.
CHESTERS
Old English 'Roman fort' - see *Chester le Street*, above. The Roman name for their fort here was *CILURNUM*, which seems to have been a reference to a cauldron - perhaps the large pool in the Tyne just outside the fort site. The first name given to the place by the later Saxons was SHUTTLECHESTER, 'Roman fort with a barred enclosure'.
CHESWICK
Old English 'cheese farm', the same as *Chiswick*, in London and the Viking *Keswick*, in Cumbria.
CHEVELEY
Old English 'Cifa's clearing'. Cifa also gave his name to nearby *Chevington*; see below.
CHEVINGTON
Old English 'farmstead of Cifa's people'. There are three; EAST, WEST and CHEVINGTON DRIFT, from the old drift mine there.
CHEVIOT
This evocative name was first recorded in 1182 as *Chiuiet*, and is almost certainly of ancient Celtic origin. Unfortunately, its meaning remains obscure. The single hill of Great Cheviot has bestowed its name on the surrounding Cheviot Hills.
CHEW GREEN
I can find no explanation for this name.
CHIBBURN
Old English 'Cilla's stream'.
CHILLINGHAM
Old English 'homestead of Ceofel's people'.
CHILTON
A Saxon name meaning 'the child's farmstead'. A Saxon 'child' was not, however, any youngster; the word usually referred to a young man who had not quite achieved 'knighthood', or perhaps to a young courtly retainer. There are at least four, including GREAT CHILTON, WEST CHILTON and CHILTON MOOR.
CHIPCHASE
This unusual name seems to be derived from Old English words meaning 'a heap of logs'. The structure in question may have been an animal trap.
CHIRDON
There are two possibilities here, both derived from Old English: 'valley with (or belonging to) a church' or 'valley with a bendy stream'.
CHIRTON
Old English *Cyrictun*. *Cyric* is related to *kirk* and *church*; the name means 'farmstead with a church'. Nearby is WEST CHIRTON.

CHOLLERFORD
This is either 'Ceola's ford' or 'ford in a gorge', both Old English.
CHOLLERTON
Old English 'farmstead near Chollerford'. See *Chollerford*, above.
CHOPPINGTON
Old English 'farmstead of Ceabba's people'.
CHOPWELL
Early written forms of this name are unclear; it may be 'Ceopa's spring', or 'spring where commerce took place' (from the Saxon *ceapian*, 'to buy and sell', which occurs in many place-names as *Chipping*, and in street-names like *Cheapside*).
CHRISTON BANK
Christon seems to be derived ultimately from an ancient Celtic word for 'hill', with *-ton* added by later Saxon settlers; 'farmstead on a hill'. Later still, Viking settlers added *Bank*.
CLAREWOOD
Old English 'farmstead enclosure in clover'.
CLAXHEUGH
Old English/Old Danish 'Clac's headland'. *Heugh* (pronounced *hyuff*) is a not uncommon local word for a headland or promontory. *Clac* was, incidentally, a Scandinavian nickname, meaning 'lump, clod'!
CLAXTON
Old English 'Clac's farmstead'.
CLEADON
Early written forms of this name - *Clevedon, Cleveton, Clyvedon, Cleveden* - have ensured confusion over its meaning. The first part is Old English *clif*, 'steep bank'. If the second part is *dun*, we have 'hill with a steep bank' (which seems

unlikely). If it is *denu*, we have 'valley with a steep bank'. And if it is *tun*, we have 'farmstead on a steep bank'.

CLEATLAM
Seems to be descended from Old English *cleat-leah*, 'clearing where burdock grows'

CLENNELL
Old English 'clean hill'. *Clean* here means 'free from harmful plants'.

CLEVELAND
First recorded in the 12th century as *Clivelanda;* it is Old English 'hilly district', and originally referred only to what we now call the CLEVELAND HILLS. *Hills* was added later by Viking invaders who did not understand the meaning of *Cleveland*. Thus we have the tautological 'hilly district hills'.

> The County of Cleveland was formed in 1974 out of the old county borough of Teesside with the addition of the areas around Hartlepool (taken from County Durham), Redcar and Guisborough (both taken from the North Riding of Yorkshire). The new name seems to have been singularly inappropriate, firstly because the County is mostly very flat, and secondly because the Cleveland Hills lie almost entirely outside it. The county was abolished in 1996.

CLIFTON
A common place-name throughout England, this is Old English 'farmstead on a steep bank'.

COALCLEUGH
Old English 'coaly ravine'.

COANWOOD
Middle English 'Collan's wood'. *Collan* was a mediaeval provost of Hexhamshire.

COATHAM
Old English 'at the cottage'.

> COATHAM MUNDEVILLE was *Cotum Maundevill* in the 14th century. *Mundeville* was added because the land here was held by one Thomas de Amundvilla, whose namesake sold it in 1274. This name itself comes from *Mondeville* in Normandy.

COCKEN
Of uncertain origin, although early written forms suggest it may be Old English 'Cocca's stream'.

COCKERTON
Old English 'farmstead on the Cocker'. Cockerton stands beside the COCKER BECK. Like the names of many other local streams and rivers, this name may be very ancient indeed. It may pre-date the Roman occupation, going back to a Celtic (Old British) word meaning 'crooked'.

COCKFIELD
Old English 'Cocca's open land'.

36

COCKLAW

Old English *cocc-hlaw*, 'wild bird hill'. Nearby runs the COCKLAW BURN.

COCKLE (PARK)

Old English *cocc-hyll*, 'wild bird hill' - the same meaning as *Cocklaw*, above.

COLDCOATS

Old English 'cold cottages'.

COLDWELL

Old English 'cold stream'.

COLLIERLEY

Old English 'charcoal-burners' clearing'.

COLWELL

This Old English name may mean the same as *Coldwell*, above - 'cold stream' - or signify a 'coaly stream'.

CONCANIS

See *CHESTER LE STREET*, above, and *The Romans and Place-Names* in the Digest.

CONISCLIFFE

Ciningesclif in the eighth century. It is Old English 'king's cliff'. The identity of the king in question is not known, though local tradition maintains it may have been Eric Bloodaxe.

There are two settlements here; HIGH and LOW CONISCLIFFE.

CONSETT

The first part part of this name may be over twenty centuries old; it has perhaps unsurprisingly undergone several changes in that time. It is thought to have started life as an Old British (Celtic) word like *cunuc*, meaning 'hilltop'. To the Saxons, who arrived much later, this was of course meaningless, so they added Old English *heafod*, 'hilltop'. Thus, in the thirteenth century, the name is written as *Conkesheved* - 'hilltop hilltop'! The present form of the name arose only fairly recently - in the fifteenth century.

CO-OPERATIVE VILLAS

A much-depleted 19th century settlement; the name may refer to a 'workers' co-operative' established to build the houses here.

COPLEY

Appears to be from Old English 'Coppa's land'.

COPT HILL

A 'copped hill' - a hill with a *copp*, 'summit'.

COQUET *(River)*

This unusual name has a rather eccentric history. Originally Old English *Cocwudu*, it was not the name of a river at all, but of a forest lying by it - 'wood of wild birds' (cock-wood). The valley in which the forest lay became *Cocwud-dael*, 'valley of the wood of wild birds'. As COQUETDALE, it, in turn, gave its name to the river in the valley - the Coquet. This process, by which a river takes its name from the

37

valley through which it flows (rather than the other way round, which is much more usual) is known as 'back-formation'. It may also have occurred at *Baldersdale* - see above.

Offshore from the mouth of the river is COQUET ISLAND.

CORBRIDGE

Ultimately, this little town just south of Hadrian's Wall owes its name to the fort which the Romans built nearby (at CORCHESTER) and which they called *CORIOSOPITUM* or *CORSTOPITUM*. The meaning of this name is unknown, but the first part of it was preserved when later Saxon settlers renewed the bridge here.

CORIOSOPITUM

See *CORBRIDGE*, above, and *The Romans and Place-Names* in the Digest.

CORNFORTH

Appears as *Corneford* in 1196, and is Old English 'cranes' ford' ('ford where there are cranes'). Nearby there is also WEST CORNFORTH.

CORNHILL

This is Old English 'cranes' nook' - so no corn and no hill are involved here.

CORNSAY

First recorded as *Corneshowe* in 1183. It is Old English 'cranes' heugh, spur of land'. There are two Cornsays; the original hilltop village, now locally referred to as OLD CORNSAY, and, some two miles east, the depleted pit village of CORNSAY COLLIERY.

CORSENSIDE

Old English 'Crossan's shelter'. *Crossan* was an Irish name.

CORSTOPITUM

See *CORBRIDGE*, above, and *The Romans and Place-Names* in the Digest.

COTHERSTONE

Cudrestune in Domesday Book. It is Old English 'Cuthere's farmstead'.

COULBY NEWHAM

Coulby seems to be Viking 'farm where charcoal was burnt'. *Newham* - 'new homestead' - will have been added when the original farm was moved to a new location, or when a new farm was built near it.

COUNDON

'The origin of this name is uncertain; it could be descended from Old English *cuna dun*, 'cow's hill'. As well as the original settlement, there are three other Coundons. NEW COUNDON is a development of the industrial age; COUNDONGATE marks the site of an historic gate into Auckland Park, and COUNDON GRANGE is a hamlet around a farm of that name.

COUPLAND

This is Old Norse *kaupland*, 'bought land'.

COWBAR

Seems to be Middle English 'gate where cows were tolled'.

38

COWDEN
First recorded as *Colden* in 1286, this is Old English 'charcoal-burners' valley'.
COWPEN
Middle English 'the coops'. In this case, a coop was probably a wickerwork device erected to catch fish. A different meaning applies at *Cowpen Bewley*, above. Local people pronounce the name *coopn*.
COWSHILL
Seems to be a late Old English/Old Danish name; 'cows hill'.
COXGREEN
Old English *cocc*, 'cock' and *coc*, 'cook' were both used as personal names, and whichever was involved here, this was his 'green', or pasture land.
COXHOE
Old English *cocc*, 'cock' and *coc*, 'cook' were both used as personal names, and whichever was involved here, this was his *hoh*, 'heugh, spur of land'.
CRAGHEAD
Seems to be Old English 'at the top of the rock (or cliff)'.
CRAGSIDE
Middle English 'hillside by a crag'.
CRAMLINGTON
May be Old English 'farmstead by the cranes' spring' or - less likely - 'of Cram's people'.
CRASTER
Started life as Old English *Crowchester*, 'Roman fort inhabited by crows'. The Latin name of the fort here is not known.
CRAWCROOK
First recorded in 1130 as *Crawecroca*. It combines Old English 'crow' with Old Norse 'crook, bend', and means 'the bend frequented by crows'; the bend in question seems to be in the road.
CRAWLEY (Northumberland)
Old English 'crows' hill'.
CRAWLEYSIDE (County Durham)
Crawley is either 'crows hill spur' or 'crows clearing'. *Side*, 'hillside', was added later.
CRESSWELL
Old English 'stream where water-cress grows'.
CRIMDON
Old English *Crumedene*, 'crooked valley'. The locally-used *Crimdon Dene* is tautological - 'crooked valley valley'.
CRONKLEY FELL
Old Norse 'fell' (moor) with Old English 'crooked cliff'.
CROOK
A Viking name which comes to us via Middle English *crok*, 'a bend', from Old

Norse *krokr*. The bend referred to may either be in the River Wear or - more likely - in Crook Beck, which flows through the town.

CROOKGATE BANK
A Viking name; 'bank on the crooked road'.

CROOKHAM
Old Norse 'at the bends' (of the River Till; for *Till*, see below).

CROOKHOUSE
Old Norse '(house at) the bends'.

CROSSGATE MOOR
A late Middle English name; 'moor near Crossgate'. *Crossgate* is Old Norse 'road to the cross'. The cross in question is Neville's Cross (which see below), erected near its present site in the 14th century.

CROXDALE
Old English '*Croc's taegl*'. *Taegl* - Modern English 'tail' - was used to denote a piece of land jutting out from a larger plot.

CULLERCOATS
No colours and no coats are involved here; the name was *Culvercoats* in about 1600. *Culver* is Old English 'pigeon, dove'; the name means 'dove-cots'.

CUSHAT LAW
Old English 'hill of wood-pigeons'.

DADDRY SHIELD
Seems to be 'Daudry's shieling (hut, shelter)'.

DALTON
Old English *dael tun*, 'farmstead in a valley'. There are two:

> DALTON LE DALE When the meaning of *Dalton* had been forgotten, the distinguishing *le Dale* - which means 'in a valley' - was added. Thus *Dalton le Dale* means 'farmstead in a valley in a valley'. Other tautological names are given in the Digest;
> DALTON PIERCY The distinguishing *Piercy* commemorates the Percy family, who held land here until 1370.

DARLINGTON
This was *Dearthingtun* in about 1050; it is Old English 'farmstead of Deornoth's people'. The central sound had changed, under Norman influence (they found *th* in this position difficult to pronounce), to *n* (*Dearningtun*) and then to *l* by the mid-twelfth century.

DARRAS HALL
In mediaeval times, the settlement here was part of the manor of Callerton (see above), and was originally known as *Callerton Darras*. The suffix is a corruption of the Norman landowner's surname; Wydo d'Araynis held the land here in 1360. Over time, *d'Araynis* has become *Darras*, the reference to Callerton was dropped, and *Hall* was added with the construction of a stone house here.

DAWDON
This name presents considerable difficulties; the village is near *Dalton* le Dale, and also nearby are the ruins of *Dalden* Tower, which matches the eleventh century spelling of the name as *Daldene*. The likeliest explanation is that Dawdon is an elliptical form of *Dalton-denu*, 'Dalton dene, valley near Dalton'.

DEAF HILL
The name commonly used by local people when referring to the mining village of *TRIMDON STATION* (see Trimdon, below). It remains obstinately inexplicable.

DEANHAM
Old English *denum*, 'at the valleys'.

DEBDON
Old English 'deep valley'; the same as *Dipton*, below.

DEERNESS *(River)*
Like the names of many local rivers and streams, *Deerness* is very ancient, dating from pre-Roman Celtic times The *deer-* part of the name is related to Welsh *dwfr*, 'river' (like the River *Dee*). The second element is probably identical with *Ness*, the name of a Scottish river. *Deerness* is thus 'River Ness'. The river gave its name to *DEERNESS VIEW*, a modern hamlet in its upper valley.

DELVES
Seems to be Old English '(at the) ditches'. It may also refer to a mine or quarry.

DENTON
Old English *den-tun*, 'farmstead in a valley'. There are at least three, including EAST and WEST DENTON.

DENWICK
Old English 'dairy farm in a valley'. The name is pronounced *dennick*.

DEPTFORD
Seems to be Old English 'deep ford'.

DERE STREET
The Roman province of *Deira* roughly occupied what is now Yorkshire. The road built from there to Hadrian's Wall was later called *Dere Street* by the Saxons - 'the Roman road from Deira'. Part of its route is still used by modern traffic; north from Piercebridge, and again between Medomsley and Ebchester. About 400yds of the road runs north from the hilltop at Brusselton as a 'hollow way', and the road itself can be seen within the remains of the fort at Binchester.

DERWENT *(River)*
The names of many local rivers and streams are of Celtic (Welsh) origin. *Derventio* was the ancient British name of this river; it is thought to be related to Modern Welsh *derw*, 'oak', and to mean 'river where oaks grow'.

DETCHANT
This name is a slight corruption of Middle English 'ditch end'; that is, the end of the ditch (or dyke).

DEVIL'S WATER *(River)*
The devil has nothing whatever to do with this little river - at least, not as far as its
name is concerned. The true derivation, however, is open to argument. *Devil's*
may be derived from two ancient Celtic words meaning 'black stream', which
also gave us *Dawlish* in Devon; *Water* would, in this case, have been added by
later Saxon settlers. Alternatively, this could be 'the stream of the d'Eiville's'
who were the 13th century landowners here.

DILSTON
Old English 'farmstead on Devil's Water' - see above.

DINNINGTON
This Old English name may mean either 'farmstead of Dunn's people' or 'farmstead
of the people on the hill'.

DINSDALE, LOW
The meaning of this name is uncertain; even the derivations of each of the two
elements - *dins* and *dale* - are the subject of heated disagreement. It has been
suggested that *Dins-* may be 'Dane's' ('belonging to a Dane') or 'Dene's' or even
'Deighton's' (that is, 'belonging to Deighton', a village over the River Tees in
North Yorkshire). Early written forms of the name show that modern *dale* is not
involved here. Instead, the ending could mean 'heugh', or be descended from Old
English *halh*, 'nook, corner'. Perm any two.

DIPTON
First appears as *Depeden*, and is Old English 'deep valley' - the same as *Debdon*,
above.

DIRT POT
Seems to be Middle English 'dirty pool', from a mediaeval local dialect word *pott*,
'pool'.

DISSINGTON
Old English 'farmstead by the ditch'. The ditch in question could be that of the
Roman Wall, which lies about two miles away.

DITCHBURN
Old English 'stream in a ditch'.

DODDINGTON
Old English 'farmstead of Dudda's people'.

DOLLAND
May be late Old English 'land of doves'.

DON *(River)*
An ancient British, pre-Roman river name; it is related to *Danube*, and is said to
be descended from a very old word for 'water'.

DORMANSTOWN
Established in 1918 as a company town for *Dorman* Long, local bridge
constructors and steelmakers. The original plan for the settlement was never
fully realised.

DOTLAND
Old Norse 'Dot's land'.
DOWNHAM
Old English *dunum*, 'at the hills'.
DOXFORD
Old English 'Docc's ford'.
DRAGONVILLE
Developed, in the late nineteenth century, around *The George and Dragon* pub, now converted.
DRURIDGE
Old English 'dry ridge'.
DUDDO
Old English 'Dudda's hill-spur'.
DUDDOE
Old English 'Dudda's valley'.
DUDLEY
Probably Old English 'Dudda's clearing'.
DUNSTAN
Old English 'stone on a hill'. The stone may have been an important boundary marker. On the coast nearby is the site of an ancient earthwork; DUNSTANBURGH ('fortification near Dunstan') was overbuilt with a castle - now an evocative ruin - in the 13th century.
DUNSTON
Seems to be Old English 'Dunn's farmstead'. Then as now, *Dunn* meant 'brown', and was used as a personal name.
DURHAM
Early written forms of the name show that it is clearly descended from Old English *dun*, 'hill' and Old Norse *holmr*, 'island'; *dun-holm*, 'hill-island'. The sound change in the middle - from *n* to *r* - is quite arbitrary; the Normans did not like a central *n*-sound. The hamlet of OLD DURHAM lies slightly to the east of the City.

> The County of Durham came into existence in 1836 - comparatively late among the canon of English counties. Before that date, the words *COUNTY DURHAM* were used in contradistinction to *North Durham*, the 'detached' parts of the Bishop's see, later absorbed into Northumberland.

EACHWICK
Apparently Old English 'dairy farm by oak-trees'.
EARLE
Local pronunciation of this name - *yerl* - goes some way in revealing its origins. In 1242, it was recorded as *Yherdhill*, Old English 'yard-hill, hill with an enclosure'.
EARSDON
Old English 'Eanred's (or Eored's) hill'

EASINGTON (County Durham/Cleveland)

Old English *Esingas-tun*, 'the farmstead of Esi's people'. Although the larger Easington (in County Durham) is one place, local usage distinguishes between the two parts of this regionally important centre. The ancient Saxon hilltop site is EASINGTON VILLAGE; the part which developed much later around the pit is EASINGTON COLLIERY.

EASINGTON (Northumberland)

Possibly Old English 'farmstead of the dwellers by the Yese'. It is supposed that *Yese* was the name of the stream by which the settlement stands. If so, the name may be Old English 'gushing, surging', or may be derived from an ancient Celtic word meaning 'boiling, seething', like the *Ouse Burn* further south - see below.

EASINGTON LANE

A colliery village so-named because it straddles about a mile of the old lane from Hetton to Easington.

EASTERSIDE

Seems to be Middle English 'hillside to the east'.

EASTGATE

Marks the place where the 'east gate' into the Prince Bishop's Weardale hunting park once stood. It is a Modern English name; the grounds were fenced and gated in the 15th century. There is also *WESTGATE*.

EBCHESTER

The Roman name for their fort here was *VINDOMORA*, said to mean 'bright waters'. Much later Saxon settlers called the place *Ebbecestr*, 'the Roman fort (*ceastre*) of Ebba'.

EDINGTON

Old English 'farmstead of Ida's people'.

EDLINGHAM

Old English 'homestead of Eadwulf's people'. Many local people pronounce the name *edlinjm*.

EDMONDSLEY

Early forms of the name make interpretation difficult. The first part may mean 'shepherd' (Old English *edemann*) or 'Eadu's man'. The terminal is *leah*, 'a clearing'.

EDMUNDBYERS

Perhaps unsurprisingly, Old English 'Eadmund's byres'.

EGGLESCLIFFE

May be Old English 'Ecca's cliff' or 'church cliff' (from a retained Celtic word for a church - *ecles*). The nearby railway junction is called *EAGLESCLIFFE*, either for reasons of sonority, or under the mistaken impression that the place-name was connected with eagles.

EGGLESTON

Appears to be Old English 'Ecgwulf's (or Ecgel's) farmstead'.

44

EGLINGHAM

Old English 'homestead of Ecwulf's people'. Many local people pronounce the name *eglinjm*.

EIGHTON BANKS

Early written forms of the name suggest that it may mean 'oak (or perhaps 'Egha's') farmstead'; *Banks* presumably from the many banks which lead to it.

ELAND

Old English *ealand*, 'island'. The settlement is really LITTLE ELAND.

ELDON

Old English 'Aella's hill'.

ELEMORE

May be Old English 'Aella's moor'.

ELFORD

Old English 'Ella's ford' or 'ford near elders'.

ELLINGHAM

Old English 'homestead of Ella's people'. Many local people pronounce the name *elinjm*.

ELLINGTON

Old English 'farmstead of Ella's people'.

ELLISHAW

Old English 'Illa's wood'.

ELRINGTON

Old English 'farmstead of alders'.

ELSDON

Old English 'Elli's valley'.

ELSTOB

Early forms of the name - *Ellestobbe, Ellestob* - suggest it means either 'elder stump' (the stump of an elder tree) or 'Aella's stump (or post)' - perhaps, in either case, a boundary marker.

ELSWICK

Old English 'Aelfsige's dairy farm'.

ELTON

Appears, in almost exactly this form, in 1090, and is usually taken to mean 'eel farmstead'; that is, a farmstead where eels were plentiful (although it may also mean the same as the many other *Eltons* in England - 'Aella's farmstead').

ELTRINGHAM

Old English 'homestead of Aelfhere's people'. Many local people pronounce the name *eltrinjm*.

ELVET

The earliest written form of this name suggests a meaning either of 'swan stream' or 'swan island'. The original Saxon settlement was probably where Durham Prison is now; part of the mediaeval manor house of Elvet Hallgarth survives there. The street leading from the nearest river crossing - Elvet Bridge - to this village was for centuries called *Old Elvet*. Ironically, when Georgian and Victorian Durham began to develop from the bridgehead in another direction, a new street was built and called *Old Elvet*, while the old street was demolished, rebuilt and called *New Elvet*!

ELWICK
Old English 'Ella's dairy farm'. There are two.

ELYHAUGH
Old English 'alder water-meadow'.

EMBLETON (County Durham)
Appears as *Elmedene* in 1190; it is Old English 'elm valley'.

EMBLETON (Northumberland)
An Old English name which may mean either 'Aemele's hill' or 'hill infested with caterpillars'. *Aemele* was, in fact, a nickname meaning 'caterpillar'.

EPPLETON
Old English 'apple valley'.

ERRING (BURN)
Like many others, the name of this stream is of very ancient, Celtic, origin; it means 'bright as silver'.
> By the stream is ERRINGTON, 'farmstead on the Erring'.

ESCOMB (ESCOMBE)
The earliest written form of this name is *Ediscum*, which seems to mean 'at the enclosed pastures' - although there is some disagreement about this.

ESH
Derived from the Old English word for an ash tree - *aesc*.
> Nearby is the colliery village of ESH WINNING; mined coal or quarried stone is often referred to as having been 'won' from the earth, and the site of extraction as a 'winning'. This village, though, seems to be the only one in England to use the word as part of its name.

ESHOTT
Old English *aesc-sceat*, 'ash-tree grove'.

ESLINGTON
Old English 'farmstead of Esla's people'.

ESPERLEY
This Old English name may be 'east of the burnt clearing' or 'aspen tree clearing'.

ESPERSHIELDS
Old English '(the place) east of Burntshiel'. For *Burntshiel*, see above.

ESPLEY
Old English 'aspen-tree clearing' (like one of the possible meanings of *Esperley*, above).

ESTON
Old English 'farmstead to the east', 'eastern farmstead'.

ETAL
This unusual name is Old English, and may mean either 'Eata's little nook' or 'nook used for grazing'.
ETHERLEY
Seems to be Old English 'Aethred's clearing'. Nearby is HIGH ETHERLEY.
ETTERSGILL
Probably Old Norse 'Etard's narrow valley (*gill*)'.
EVENWOOD
Old English 'even (level) wood'.
EWART
Old English *ea-worth*, 'farmstead enclosure by a river'.
EWESLEY
First recorded as *Oseley* in 1286, this is probably Old English 'blackbird clearing'.
FAIRHAUGH
Old English 'fair (pleasant) water-meadow'.
FALLOWDON and FALLODON
Old English 'fallow (yellow) hill'.
FALLOWFIELD
The name is Old English and may mean either 'fallow (yellow) field' or 'newly-cultivated pasture'.
FALLOWLEES
Old English 'newly-cultivated clearing'. The settlement gave its name to FALLOWLEES BURN.
FALSTONE
Seems to be Old English 'multi-coloured stone'. The stone may have been used as a boundary or meeting-place marker.
FAREWELL HALL
May well have got its evocative name from its location at the edge of Durham City, where the old Great North Road passed southward into open country.
FARNE ISLANDS
The name seems to derive from Old English *fearn*, 'fern', though it is difficult to see why. Unexpectedly, though, the name is certainly not related to nearby *Lindisfarne*; see below.
FARNHAM
The name is deceptive; it started life as Old English *thirnum*, 'at the thorn-trees'.
FARNLEY
Old English 'ferny clearing'.
FATFIELD
Early references to this name are rare. The settlement developed as a mining village in the nineteenth century, probably on a green field site, and may have used the name given by the farmer to his field; 'fat' has been used in this way for centuries to mean 'richly fertile'.

FAWDINGTON
Old English 'farmstead where animals were folded'.
FAWDON
Old English 'multicoloured hill'.
FAWNLEES
First appears as *Fawleys*, and is descended from Old English words meaning 'multi-coloured clearing'.
FAWNS
Old English 'multicoloured'.
FAWSIDE
Contains the same Old English word as *Fawnlees* and *Fawns* above, and means 'multi-coloured slope'.
FEATHERSTONE
Old English *feotherstan*, 'four stones'. The name refers to a tetralith or cromlech consisting of three upright stones and a cross-head stone; one of these structures must have stood here in ancient times.
FELKINGTON
Old English 'farmstead of Feoluca's people'.
FELLGATE
Gate here is 'road', and *fell* is used - as often in this area - to mean a low-lying moor; so this is Old Norse 'the road to the fell'.
FELLING
Descended either from Old English *faelging*, 'newly-cultivated land' or from Middle English *felling*, 'a clearing' (from *faelle*, 'to fell (trees, shrubs))'. Interestingly, many local people refer to the place as *the* Felling.
FELTON
Old English 'Fygla's farmstead'.
FENCEHOUSES
Unsurprisingly, 'houses by a fence'. The name seems to be comparatively modern.
FENHAM
Earliest spellings of this name are confusing. It may be 'at the fens', or perhaps 'water-meadow (*hamm*) by the fen', both Old English.
FENROTHER
Old English 'clearing with a heap of wood'.
FENTON
Old English 'farmstead by a fen'.
FENWICK
Old English 'dairy farm by a fen'.

Felton, Northumberland
10 miles north of Morpeth

FERRYHILL

Written forms of this name do not occur until comparatively late - in the fourteenth and fifteenth centuries - and are confusing; various explanations have been proposed. However, it is likely that the name is descended from Old English *fiergen*, 'wooded hill'. In any case, ferries are certainly not involved. FERRYHILL STATION is a separate industrial settlement about 1m east.

FINCHALE

Pronounced *finkle*; seems to be Old English 'finch nook, nook frequented by finches'. although it is possible that the finches frequented a 'heugh' (headland) rather than a 'nook'.

FINDON HILL
The name is tautological - it says the same thing twice. *Findon* is 'hill with a heap of wood'. *Hill* was added later, when the meaning of *Findon* was forgotten; thus the full meaning is 'hill with a heap of wood hill'. See the Digest for other tautological names.

FIR TREE
There are at least three possible explanations for this name. It may refer, as it most obviously suggests, to an important - perhaps boundary-marking - fir tree. This seems, however, unlikely; such a usage would be Anglo-Saxon, and fir trees were introduced to Britain later - the word does not seem to have been used in Old English, in which language the name probably meant something like 'Faer's tree' (on the same pattern as *Picktree*, below). Finally, the name may also commemorate an inn - *The Fir Tree* - which may have stood here in mediaeval times.

FISHBURN
Perhaps unsurprisingly, Old English 'fish stream, stream with plenty of fish'.

FLASS
Descended from an Old French word *flasque*, 'pool, boggy land', taken into Middle English as *flask* or *flasshe*. The word occurs elsewhere in the area, as at *FLASS VALE*, part of Durham City. *Flash* is still used locally in England to mean a small pool or lake.

FLEETHAM
Old English 'homestead by a stream (fleet).'

FLEMINGFIELD
This part of Shotton was granted to John de *Flemyng* - 'of Flanders' - in 1382.

FLINT HILL
May be Old Norse 'hill where flints were found'.

FLODDEN
Although undoubtedly an Old English name, *Flodden* was not recorded until as recently as 1513, when the battle was fought here. It may denote 'hill by a stream'.

FLOTTERTON
The name was first recorded as *Flotweyton* in 1160, and seems to be Old English 'float-way-farmstead'; that is, a farmstead by a 'floating' road, perhaps a road built on rafts of some kind.

FONT *(River)*
The meaning of this ancient Celtic name is unknown.

FORD
Old English 'ford'.

FOREST HALL
Originally the home of a 'forester', the mediaeval 'gamekeeper' of the forested estates of the Lord of the Manor. The name is comparatively recent; *forest* came

into Middle English from Old French after the Conquest.

FOREST IN TEESDALE

Self-explanatory. For a note about *forest*, see *Forest Hall*, above.

FORTHERLEY

Old English 'clearing of the sheep-herders'.

FOURSTONES

Old English 'four stones'. Perhaps they had the same significance as those at *Featherstone* seem to have done; see above.

FOWBERRY

Old English 'fortification where foals were kept'.

FOXTON

First appears as *Foxedene* in 1170, and is Old English 'fox valley'.

FRAMLINGTON

Old English 'farmstead of Framela's people'. There is also LONGFRAMLINGTON, from its shape.

FRAMWELLGATE

The name *Framwell* may mean 'the strong (vigorous) spring', or may denote that the spring belonged to someone called Fram. *Gate* is Old Norse *gata*, 'street'; this is 'the street to Framwell'.

FROSTERLEY

Forsterlegh in 1239, this is 'the forester's clearing'; *forester* is from Old French, *legh* is from Old English *leah*.

FULTHORPE

The second part is descended from Old English *throp*, the precise meaning of which is uncertain. It may have meant 'dependent farm' or even 'hamlet'. The first part may mean 'foul, dirty', or may refer to someone called *Fulla* or *Folga*.

FULWELL

Old English 'foul, dirty stream'.

GAINFORD

Opinions differ as to the meaning of the earliest forms of this name; it may either be 'direct (straight) ford' or 'Gaega's ford' - both Old English.

GARMONDSWAY

The name of this now deserted mediaeval village is Old English 'Garmond's road' - the road said to have been used by King Cnut for his pilgrimage to the shrine of St Cuthbert.

The Angel of the North, Gateshead

GATESHEAD
There seem to be three very different possibilities here. Firstly, the name may signify 'the end of the road' (before the river crossing) from Old Norse *gata*, 'road'. It is more likely, though, that Gateshead is really 'goat's head'. This could, of course, refer simply to a 'headland frequented by wild goats'. However, it is known that animal and human sacrifice was widespread in England in late Saxon times - several other place-names commemorate the fact - and Gateshead could be the site of a totemised sacrificial 'goat's head'.

GAUNLESS *(River)*
This is Middle English *gaghenles*, which is descended from an Old Norse word meaning 'useless' - although why this river, as opposed to any other, should be so-named is a matter of conjecture!

GIBSIDE
Of uncertain origin; it may be Old English 'Gyppa's (sheep)fold'.

GILESGATE
Middle English 'road to St Giles' church (and parish)'.

GILMONBY
Old Norse 'Gilman's farm'.

GILSLAND
Seems to be Old Norse 'Gilla's land'.

GLANTLEES
The name seems to be derived from a Viking, Middle English word for 'look-out'. Nearby is *Glantlees Hill*, 'look-out hill'.

GLANTON
Seems to be derived from the same source as *Glantlees*, above; 'farmstead with a look-out'. Nearby is the hill of *Glanton Pike*.

GLEN *(River)*
Like many river-names, *Glen* is descended form an ancient British word, here meaning 'clean, holy, beautiful'. Its valley is GLENDALE.

GLENDUE
An ancient name, derived from Old Welsh *glyn-du*, 'dark valley'.

GOSFORTH
Old English 'goose ford, ford where there were geese'. Nearby is SOUTH GOSFORTH.

GOSWICK
Old English 'goose farm'. The name is pronounced *gozik*.

GRANGETOWN
'The township around the grange'; the name is modern.

GRANGE VILLA
This sonorous name seems to have started life as *Grangeville*, the name given to the new mining village when the pit was sunk in the 1850s. Previously, the only house here had been Pelton *Grange*. See also *PELTON*, below.

GRAYTHORP
Started life as an 'unofficial' name adopted by local people for this area after Sir William Gray opened a shipyard here in 1913.

GREATHAM
The earliest written forms of this Old English name make interpretation difficult. It may be *great-ham*, 'large homestead', *greot-ham*, 'sandy (or gravelly) homestead', or even *grith-ham*, 'peaceful homestead'. The name is pronounced *greethm*.

GREENHAUGH
Old English 'green water-meadow'.

GREENHEAD
Old English 'green hilltop'.

GRETA *(River)*
Old Norse 'stoney stream'. There are three rivers of this name in the Pennines, and there is a River *Griota* in Iceland. The river has given its name to the hamlet of GRETA BRIDGE. The Roman fort of *MORBIUM* (whose meaning is unknown) may have been situated here, or at *Piercebridge*, further east.

GRINDON
Old English 'green hill'.

GUIDE POST

An esoteric name with a simple explanation. The settlement grew up around a signpost - and public house - which stood at this once important crossroads.

GUISBOROUGH

A Viking name, first recorded as *Gighesburg* and *Gighesborc* in Domesday Book. The second part is Old Norse 'fortified place', but the precise meaning of the first element is unknown. For some purposes, the name is spelt *Gisborough*.

GUNNERTON

Old English 'Gunnward's farmstead'.

GUYZANCE

Recorded as *Gysnes* in 1254, this unusual name is manorial; it refers to the family name - *Guines* -of the Norman landlords of this area. Their name is, in turn, derived from their French home town of *Guines*, near Calais.

HABITANCUM

See *Risingham*, below, and *The Romans and Place-Names* in the Digest.

HADSTONE

Old English 'Haedda's farmstead'. The name is sometimes spelt *HADSTON*.

HAGGERLEASES

Leases is Old English 'pasture lands'. *Hagger-* is more difficult to explain, though it may derive from the same source as in *Haggerston*, below.

HAGGERSTON

Middle English 'Hagard's farmstead'. *Hagard* was probably a Norman French nickname meaning 'wild, strange'.

HAINING

Derives from a local dialect word for an enclosure, originally an area of farmland fenced off to produce winter fodder. There are at least three, including HAINING HALL and HAINING RIGG, where 'rigg' is Viking 'ridge'.

HALLGARTH (PITTINGTON)

Probably a combination of Old English 'nook, corner' and Old Norse 'garth, enclosure'; 'enclosure in a nook'. Pittington Hallgarth is the site of a largely deserted mediaeval village.

HALLINGTON

First recorded in 1247 as *Halidene*, this is Old English 'holy valley'.

HALTON

Seems to be derived from Old English *haw-hyll*, 'look-out hill'. HALTON SHIELDS are 'the shelters atop Halton'.

HALTWHISTLE

Sadly, no trains are involved here. Instead, the name is Old English 'fork of a river by a hill'. The second part of the name is found elsewhere at *Twizell*; see below.

HAMILTON ROW

This small mining village seems to have taken its name from that of the first terrace built here.

HAMSTEELS

The first part is Old English *ham*, 'homestead'. The second is less easy to interpret; it may be *steal*, 'a stall, cattle shed' or perhaps *stigol*, 'steep bank' - 'homestead on a steep hill'.

HAMSTERLEY

The first part seems to come from the Old English word for a corn-weevil; the name means 'corn-weevil clearing'.

HARBOTTLE

Old English 'dwelling for the hirelings' or 'of the army', though which army this may have been is unknown.

HARDWICK

A fairly common name throughout England; it is Old English 'sheep farm' - *heordwic*.

HAREHAUGH

No hares here. This is Old English 'water-meadow by an old fort'.

HAREHOPE

Old English 'hare valley'.

HARELAW

Seems to be Old English 'boundary hill'.

HARLE

The name seems to be a rare reference to paganism; Old English 'clearing of the heathen temple'. The settlement is divided into KIRKHARLE ('with a church') and LITTLE HARLE.

HARLOW HILL

Harlow is here probably Old English *here-hlaw*, 'hill of the people'. Perhaps this was an ancient meeting-place. In any case, *hill* was added later when the meaning of *Harlow* had been forgotten; thus we have 'hill of the people hill'.

HARNHAM

Seems to be Old English 'rocky homestead'.

HARPERLEY

A fairly unusual example of an 'occupational' place-name; it is Old English 'clearing of the harper' (someone who plays the harp).

HARRATON

The earliest written form of this name occurs in 1190 as *Hervertune*. The final element is Old English *tun*, 'farmstead', and the first part of the name seems to be identical with *Hereford*, which is Old English 'army ford'. This term was used to mean a large ford - one big enough for an army to cross (in this case, the River Wear). Thus *Harraton* is 'farmstead by the large ford'.

HARROWGATE

A combination of Old English *haerg*, 'heathen temple' and Old Norse *gata*, 'road' - 'the road to the heathen temple'.

HART

First recorded by Bede as *Herut-eu*, 'stag island'. Besides the obvious meaning, *island* could, at this time, also refer to land *partly* surrounded by water (which it did at Durham, *dun-holm*, 'hill island', and which it still does at, for example, *Isle* of Portland and *Isle* of Dogs). Thus the island referred to here is probably the peninsula or headland (locally called The Heugh) on which Hartlepool now stands, and which, in Saxon times, was part of the manor of Hart.

Local people refer to this place as *HART VILLAGE*, presumably in contradistinction to HART STATION, a small settlement about 1m east, which developed around the station built to serve the village. This settlement is now part of Hartlepool.

HARTBURN

Old English 'stag stream'. There are two, and an EAST HARTBURN.

HARTFORD

Old English 'stag ford'. The settlement is divided into EAST and WEST.

HARTINGTON

First recorded in 1174 as *Hertweitun* (*Hart-way-ton*), this is Old English 'farmstead by the stags' path'. This must have been a track used by deer.

HARTLAW

Old English 'stag hill'.

HARTLEPOOL

First occurs in the twelfth century variously as *Herterpol*, *Herterpul*, and *Hertelpol*. The name is descended from *Heruteu-pol*, 'the pool near Hart' - probably referring to the bay which the town almost encloses.

Until local government reorganisation in 1974, there were two quite separate towns here. The ancient Saxon settlement came to be known locally as *OLD HARTLEPOOL* while the much larger Victorian town was *WEST HARTLEPOOL*.

HARTLEY

Old English 'stag clearing'. The settlement is divided into OLD and NEW.

ˈHARTON

Hertedun, Old English 'stag hill'.

HARWOOD

An Old English name whose derivation is uncertain; it may be 'grey wood' or 'stoney wood' or 'hare's wood'. There are at least three; near one of them is HARWOOD SHIEL, 'hut by Harwood'.

HASWELL

Old English *haesel wells*, 'hazel spring'. The pit village of HASWELL PLOUGH nearby takes its name from the inn which, before the colliery was sunk here, was the only building at the small crossroads. There is also HIGH HASWELL.

HAUGHTON

Old English 'farmstead by a water-meadow'. There are at least two, including:
> HAUGHTON LE SKERNE The distinguishing *le Skerne* ('by the River Skerne') was added under Norman French influence; see *Skerne*, below.

HAUXLEY

Old English 'hawks' hill' or perhaps 'Hafoc's hill'. *Hafoc* was a nickname that meant 'the hawk'.

HAVERTON HILL

Early written forms of this name are rare; it may be Old English 'Haefa's farmstead', or 'farmstead at the headland'. The reference to 'hill' must be ironic - the land is particularly flat here!

HAWICK

Probably Old English 'high dairy farm'.

HAWKHILL

Probably Old English 'hawk hill', though this could have been 'the hill belonging to a man called Hawk'.

HAWKWELL

Old English 'hawk stream'.

HAWTHORN

As obvious as it seems - 'hawthorn'. Interestingly, Old English *haga* was 'an enclosure'; the word gradually came to mean the fence which did the enclosing - 'hedge' - and later still was applied to the type of thorn tree most commonly used for this purpose; hence 'hawthorn' is 'hedgethorn'.

HAYDON

Old English 'hay valley'. The settlement is now called HAYDON BRIDGE, 'the bridge at Haydon'.

HAZLERIGG

is probably Old Norse 'hazel ridge'.

HAZON

Early written forms of this unusual name suggest it may be Old English 'hedge end'.

HEADLAM

A form of Old English *heath-leah*, '(at the) heathery clearing'.

HEALEY

Old English 'high clearing'. There are at least three, and a HEALEYFIELD, 'pasture by a high clearing'.

HEATHERSLAW

Heather is not involved here; this is Old English 'deer hill'.

HEATHPOOL
This seems to be 'pool under Hetha'. The hill nearby is known as *Hetha*, although the meaning of this name is a mystery.

HEATON
Old English 'high farmstead'. There at least three, including CASTLE HEATON. And in central Northumberland are CAPHEATON - the meaning of *Cap-* here is uncertain, though it may indicate 'chief, main' - and KIRKHEATON, 'with a church'.

HEBBURN
Variously interpreted as 'at the broad water', or 'high tumulus' - both of them Old English. (A *tumulus* is a small, prehistoric artificial burial mound).

HEBRON
Seems to be Old English 'high tumulus', as at *Hebburn*, above.

HECKLEY
May be Old English 'high cliff' or 'heath (heathery) cliff'.

HEDDON
Old English 'heathery hill'. There are at least two settlements with this name.
>   HEDDON ON THE WALL is by Hadrian's Wall;
>   BLACK HEDDON presumably from the colour of the soil.

HEDDON, EAST and WEST
These *Heddons* are Old English 'Hidda's pasture'.

HEDGELEY
Old English 'Hidda's clearing'.

HEDLEYHOPE, EAST
Hedley is as at *HEDLEY ON THE HILL* above. *Hope* is Old English 'valley'. Thus *East Hedleyhope* is '(at the) east of the valley of the heathery clearing'. There does not appear to be a North, South or West Hedleyhope.

HEDLEY ON THE HILL
Hedley is related to *Headlam* above and means 'heathery clearing'.

HEDWORTH
Old English 'farmstead enclosure on the heath'

HEFFERLAW
Old English 'hill by the high ford'.

HEIGHINGTON
Old English 'farmstead of Heca's people'.

HELM
Seems to be the Old Norse word for 'helmet', adapted to mean a roofed cattle-shelter or shed.

HELMINGTON ROW
Helmington is Old English 'farmstead of Helm's people'. The addition of *Row* is late mediaeval, and is not uncommon in County Durham - there is also *Billy Row* and *Shiney Row*. It may mean either a row of rough cottages or shielings, or a

stretch or patch of countryside.

HEMLINGTON

Old English 'farmstead of Hymel's people'.

HENDON

Old English *hind-denu*, 'valley of hinds (deer)'.

HENSHAW

Possibly Old English 'Hethin's nook'.

HEPBURN

The exact origins of this name are unknown; it may, though, be identical in meaning with *Hebburn*, above - it is pronounced in the same way.

HEPPLE

Old English 'water-meadow where hips grow'.

HEPSCOTT

Old English 'Hebbi's cottages'.

HERRINGTON

Old English 'farmstead of Here's people'.

There are five Herringtons - EAST, MIDDLE, WEST, NEW and HERRINGTON BURN.

HESLEDEN

Old English 'hazel valley'. There are two Hesledens - HIGH HESLEDEN named for its position on a hilltop overlooking the coast, and nearby MONK HESLEDEN (the monks were those of Durham, who owned land here).

HESLEDON, COLD

Old English 'cold hazel hill'.

HETHERINGTON

Old English 'farmstead of the heath-dwellers'.

HETT

Opinion is divided as to the meaning of this deceptively simple name; it may be derived from either of two Old English words, and may thus mean either 'heath, moor', or, more likely, 'hat' (from the shape and markings of the slight hill on which it stands).

HETTON (County Durham)

Early forms of the name suggest that it means either 'Heppe's hill', or 'hill where hips grow'.

There are three Hettons. HETTON LE HOLE ('in the valley'), HETTON LE HILL ('on the hill'), and SOUTH HETTON.

HETTON (Northumberland)

Old English 'farmstead on the heath'.

HEUGH

Old English *hoh*, 'spur of land, promontory'.

HEWORTH

Old English 'high enclosed farmstead'.

HEXHAM

This name has a satisfyingly complex history and meaning. It was first recorded - as early as 681 AD - as *Hagustaldes ea*, 'stream of the Hagustald', and referred to the stream here. A few years later, *ea* was altered to *ham*, 'homestead'. Originally, Old English *hagustald* signified a warrior or bachelor, but came to mean a younger son who, having no share or land in the village, had to set an enclosure up for himself outside the settlement boundaries.

HIGHAM

Old English 'high homestead'.

HIGH FORCE

Old Norse 'high waterfall'.

HIGH GRANGE

'High grange'; the name is comparatively late.

HIGH HANDENHOLD

There is some doubt as to the origins of this striking name. It may originally have been *Handen*, Old English 'Hana's valley'. To this may have been added a local dialectal version of Viking 'hill' - 'the hill by Hana's valley'. The descriptive 'high' seems to have been a recent addition.

HIGH SPEN

Spen occurs in other place-names in the North-East - like *Spennymoor*, and *Spennithorne* in North Yorkshire. Unfortunately, its precise meaning is unknown, although it may signify 'hedge'.

HIGH STOOP

A *stoop* was a mediaeval gateway, and, at 1,000ft, this one was certainly high!

HILTON

Old English *hyll-tun*, 'farmstead on a hill'.

HINDLEY

Old English 'clearing frequented by hinds (female deer)'.

HIRST

Old English *hyrst*, 'wooded hill'. The word is much more widespread in southern England than here in the north.

HOBSON

I can find no explanation for this unusual name.

HOLBURN

Old English 'stream in a deep hollow'. The name is the same as *Holborn*, in London.

HOLE

Old English 'hollow, valley'.

HOLEYN, HOLLIN and HOLLING(S)

Old English 'holly tree'.

HOLMESIDE

Appears to be late Old English 'outlying land by water'.

HOLWICK

Old English 'dairy farm in a hollow', or 'in the holly'.

HOLY ISLAND

Because of its associations with St Aidan and St Cuthbert, the island of *Lindisfarne* (see below) had already acquired this alternative name by the 12th century. The village on the island is known *only* by this name.

HOLYSTONE

Old English 'holy stone'. The stone in question may have had religious or saintly associations.

HOLYWELL

is 'holy spring', though I have been unable to determine why the small stream here was so-named. There are two settlements here - EAST and WEST HOLYWELL.

HOPPEN

Old English 'at the valleys'; the word is a version of the second part of *Stan*hope and *Wester*hope and, slightly altered, occurs at *Wide Open* - see below.

HOPPYLAND

May be Old English 'Oppa's land', although early forms of the name are unclear.

HORDEN

First recorded in about 1050 as *Horedene*; it is Old English 'filthy (dirty, muddy) valley'.

HORNCLIFFE

Old English 'cliff in a tongue of land'.

HORSLEY
Old English 'pasture for horses'. There are three, including LONGHORSLEY (from the shape of the village) and HORSLEY HILL.

HORTON
Old English 'farmstead on muddy (dirty) land'. There are at least three, including EAST and WEST HORTON.

HOUGHALL
Pronounced *hoffl*. It occurs variously as *Howhale*, *Hocchale* and *Houhal*, and means 'nook on a heugh (hill spur)'.

HOUGHTON
Old English 'farmstead on a heugh, hill spur'. There are at least five, including LONGHOUGHTON (from the shape of the settlement), LITTLEHOUGHTON and:

> HOUGHTON LE SIDE which refers to the settlement's position on a hillside;
> HOUGHTON LE SPRING which commemorates the Spring family, who are known to have held land here in 1220.

HOUSESTEADS
Late Old English '(place of) homesteads, farms'. The Romans called their fort here *VERCOVICIUM*, which may have meant 'place of good fighters'.

HOWDEN (Northumberland)
Old English 'deep (hollow) valley'.

HOWDEN LE WEAR
Old English 'dwelling in the valley (of the Wear)'.

HOWDON
Probably Old English 'main hill', that is, the highest hill in the area.

HOWICK
Old English 'high dairy farm' - the same as *Hawick*, above.

HOWTEL
Old English 'wooded water-meadow'.

HULAM
Old English *holum*, 'in the hollow'.

HULNE
Old English 'holly'. The name is pronounced *hool*, to rhyme with 'school'.

HUMBLEDON HILL, HUMBLETON HILL
Both names are derived from Old English *haemel-dun*. *Haemel*, in place names, seemed to mean 'bare (or treeless)', or perhaps 'spoilt, misshapen'. *Dun* is 'hill'. Thus we have 'bare hill' for *Humbledon*. *Hill* was added later, when the meaning of *dun* had been forgotten. So we end up with 'bare hill hill'.

HUMMERBECK
Although *-beck* is Old Norse 'stream', I can find no explanation for *Hummer-*.

HUMSHAUGH
Old English 'Hun's water-meadow'.
HUNDERTHWAITE
Old Norse 'Hunrethr's low meadow'.
HUNSTANWORTH
Old English 'Hunstan's enclosed farmstead'.
HUNTERLEY
Old English 'huntsman's clearing'.
HUNWICK
Old English 'Huna's dairy farm'.
HURBUCK
Hurthebuck in 1303. It is thought to derive from Old Norse 'at the back of the door, the space behind the door'; what it signifies here is a mystery. The hamlet is now called *HURBUCK COTTAGES*.
HURWORTH
Old English 'farmstead enclosed with hurdles'. There are two:
> HURWORTH BRYAN was held in 1211 by Brian, son of Alan, Earl of Richmond;
> HURWORTH ON TEES is by that river. For *Tees*, see below.
HUTTON
The same as *Houghton* - 'farmstead on a heugh'. There are at least three, including:
> HUTTON HENRY Henry de Essh held the manor here in about 1380.
> HUTTON MAGNA incorporates Church Latin 'large, great'.
HYLTON
Early written forms of this name are inconclusive. It may mean 'farmstead on a hill' or 'on a slope' or 'where wild tansy grows', all from Old English. The settlement is divided into NORTH and SOUTH HYLTON by the River Wear.
ILDERTON
Old English 'farmstead amongst elders'.
INGLEBY
Old Norse 'farm of the English'. *English* here has its 'true' meaning - an Angle (as opposed to a Saxon). Other nationalities are sometimes 'earmarked' in this way - see *Flemingfield, Ireshopeburn, Shotton, Walworth.*
> INGLEBY BARWICK is 'by a barley farm'. Interestingly, this hamlet was called *Cold Ingleby* in the 13th century.
INGLETON
This Old English name has hardly changed since it was first recorded in 1050. It may mean either 'Ingeld's (or Ingwald's) farmstead' or 'farmstead of the English'. *English* here has its 'true' meaning - an Angle (as opposed to a Saxon). Other nationalities are sometimes 'earmarked' in this way - see *Flemingfield, Ireshopeburn, Shotton, Walworth.*

INGOE

Old English 'Inga's hill-spur'.

INGRAM

Old English 'grassland, pasture land'. A version of this word is found as the first part of *Angerton*, above.

INKERMAN

A modern name of the industrial era; it commemorates the Battle of Inkerman (in the Crimean War).

IRESHOPEBURN

This is 'stream (*burn*) in the valley (*hope*) of the Irish'. For other 'earmarked' foreigners, see *Ingleby, Ingleton, Shotton, Walworth* and others.

IVESLEY

May be Old English 'Ivo's clearing'.

IVESTON

Old English 'Ivo's stone'. The significance of the stone is unknown; it may have been a local boundary marker.

JARROW

The much-corrupted name of a tribe, the *Gyrwe*, who lived here in Bede's time (the 7th century). *Gyrwe* is itself derived from an Old English word for 'mud' or 'fen' - the tribe was 'the dwellers on the mudflats (or fenland)'. It is likely that the tribe migrated here from the fens of the East Midlands.

JESMOND

'At the mouth of the Ouse burn', corrupted to its present form under Norman French influence from what would otherwise have become *Ousemouth*. Nearby is WEST JESMOND.

KEARSLEY

Old English 'Cynehere's hill'.

KEEPWICK

Old English 'dairy farm where trading was carried out'. In a different form, the first part of this name can be seen in *Chopwell*; see above.

KELLOE

Derived from Old English *celf-hlaw*, 'calf hill'. Local people refer to two other Kelloes; *CHURCH KELLOE* is that part of the village near the ancient church and, about a mile away, *TOWN KELLOE* is a tiny hamlet on the site of a larger - deserted - mediaeval village.

KENTON

Old English *cyne-tun*, 'royal farmstead'. The identity of its royal Anglo-Saxon patron is unknown. Nearby KENTON BANKFOOT is self-explanatory, whilst KENTON BAR suggests that a toll bar once stood here.

KEPIER

Derived from Old English *cype-gear*. A *cype* was a sort of willow-basket used to catch fish; *gear* is 'weir'.

64

KETTLEBURN
May be Old English 'Ketil's stream' or 'stream in a narrow valley'.
KETTON
Old English 'Ceatta's farmstead'.
KIBBLESWORTH
Old English 'Cybbel's farmstead enclosure'.
KIDLAND
Old English 'Cydda's land'.
KIELDER
Originally the name of a river - now called *Kielder Burn* - this name, like those of many other rivers, is very ancient, and derives from two Old Welsh words meaning 'violent stream'. It is identical with the many rivers of northern England called *Calder*.

> The burn has been dammed to form a reservoir named, Lake District-style, KIELDER WATER.

KILHAM
Old English *cylnum*, 'at the kilns'.
KILLERBY
Old English 'Kilvert's village (or homestead)'.
KILLHOPE
May be Old English 'narrow valley'.
KILLINGWORTH
Old English 'farmstead enclosure of Cylla's people'. The area around the old village has been designated a 'new town', and Killingworth now consists of *TOWNSHIP*, *VILLAGE* and *MOOR*.
KILNPIT HILL
Middle English 'hilltop of the lime-kiln pit'.
KIMBLESWORTH
Old English 'Cynehelm's farmstead enclosure'.
KIMMERSTON
Old English 'Cynemaer's farmstead'.
KININVIE
Unfortunately, this unusual name has not, so far, been explained.
KIRKHAUGH
Old English 'water-meadow with a church'.
KIRKLEATHAM
Leatham is Old English 'on a slope'. *Kirk* - 'church' - was added later by the Vikings to distinguish this settlement from *Upleatham*, for which, see below.
KIRKLEY
This name seems to have started life as ancient Celtic *cruc*, 'hill'. Later Saxon settlers, ignorant of the name's meaning, added 'hill'. The meaning of the

compound name was forgotten over time, so that *hlaw*, another Saxon word for 'hill', was added; thus in the 13th century, the name was recorded as *Crekellawe*, 'hill hill hill'!

KIRKLEY, WHITE
Seems to mean 'white kirtle land', although the meaning of this is uncertain.

KIRKNEWTON
See *Newton*, below.

KITTY BREWSTER
Seems to be named after a local pub where Kitty the Brewster brewed her ale.

KNARESDALE
Middle English 'the valley by Knar'. *Knar* - a small settlement in the valley - seems to be Middle English 'rugged rock'.

KNITSLEY
Old English 'knight's clearing'. The knight's identity is unknown.

KYLOE
Old English *cy-leah*, 'clearing for grazing cattle'.

KYO
This striking name has a disappointingly unexotic meaning - it is Old English *cy-hoh*, 'cow hill'.

LACKENBY
The common ending *-by* is Old Norse 'farm'; the meaning of *Lacken-* is less certain, although it may refer to an Old Irish personal name *Lochan* - 'Lochan's farm'.

LAITHKIRK
I have been unable to discover the meaning of *Laith-* here.

LAMBLEY
Old English 'clearing for grazing lambs'.

LAMBTON
Old English 'farmstead where lambs were kept'.

LAMESLEY
Old English *lamba-leah*, 'lamb clearing'.

LANCHESTER
The first known settlement here was the Roman fort, the scant remains of which may still be seen. Its name was *LONGOVICIUM*, which may mean either 'place by the pool' or 'place of the ship-fighters'. Later Anglo-Saxon settlers retained the first part of the name - *long* - but seem to have interpreted it as their own word *lang*, 'long'. As usual, *ceastre* ('Roman fort') was added - *Langecestr'*, 'long Roman fort'.

LANEHEAD
'The end of the road' (through Weardale). Not far beyond this scattered settlement the road rises to cross the border into Cumbria.

LANGDON BECK
Langdon is Old English 'long hill'. *Beck* - 'burn, stream' - is a later Scandinavian addition.
LANGLEY
Old English 'long clearing'. There are at least three, including:
> LANGLEY MOOR occupies what must have been heathery, open land before colliery development;
> LANGLEY PARK commemorates the parkland of nearby Langley Hall, on which it was built.
LANGTON
Means the same as *Langdon (Beck)*, above; it is Old English 'long hill'.
LANTON
Old English 'long farmstead'.
LARTINGTON
Old English 'farmstead of Lyrti's people'.
LAWE, THE
This part of South Shields is Viking 'the hill'.
LAZENBY
Old Norse 'farm of the freedman' (someone released from serfdom).
LEADGATE
The gate here was not made of lead. The name is derived from Old English *hlidgeat*, 'swinging gate'.
LEAM, LEAMSIDE
There is some disagreement about the meaning of this name. It has been suggested that *Leam* is a version of Old English *leah*, and means '(at the) clearings'. *Leamside* would then mean 'slope at the clearings'. Another authority suggests that *Leam* is a stream name meaning 'glittering', although this is less likely.
LEARCHILD
Old English 'Leofric's slope'. The second part of the name is also found in *Akeld*, above.
LEARMOUTH
A corruption of *Levermouth*, '(at the) mouth of the River Lever'. The settlement is divided into EAST and WEST. For *Lever*, see below.
LEASES, LEAZES
Old English *laeswias*, 'pasture land'.
LEASINGTHORNE
Seems to commemorate a special thorn tree - perhaps an important boundary marker. The name probably means either 'Lesing's thorn' or (connected to *Leazes*, above) 'pasture thorn'.
LEE HALL
Middle English 'stone-built house by the clearing'.

LEIGHTON GREEN
'The pastureland by Leighton'. LEIGHTON is Old English 'bright hill'.
LEMINGTON
Old English 'farmstead where brook-lime (*hleomoc*) could be obtained'.
LESBURY
Old English 'fortified place of the leech'. This meaning is not as nonsensical as it looks; 'leech' was used by the Saxons to mean 'physician, doctor'.
LEVEN *(River)*
Like many river- and stream-names locally and nationally, this is a very ancient Celtic name which may be related to Modern Welsh *llyfn*, 'smooth'. By the river is the hamlet of HIGH LEVEN.
LEVER *(River)*
Derived from Old English 'iris, rush'.
LEVINGTON
Old English 'farmstead of Leofa's people'. There were originally two settlements here; KIRKLEVINGTON has Viking *Kirk*, 'church'. About 2m east - on the other side of the A19 trunk road - is the site of CASTLE LEVINGTON.
LILBURN
Old English 'Lilla's stream'.
LINDISFARNE
The older name of *HOLY ISLAND*; see above. It seems to mean 'island of the people from Lindsey'; perhaps a group or tribe from what is now part of north Lincolnshire moved north and settled here, as a group of fenland folk did at *JARROW* - see above. The name may also mean 'island of travellers to Lindsey', perhaps denoting a settlement of regular traders with that area. In any case, it is surprising that the close proximity of the FARNE *ISLANDS* is purely coincidental; the names are unconnected.
LINHOPE
Old English 'lime-tree valley' or 'flax valley'.
LINMOUTH
A corruption of '(at the) mouth of the River Lyne'. For *Lyne*, see below.
LINSHEELES
Old English 'huts amongst lime-trees'. The second part of the name is also found in *SOUTH SHIELDS* and many other names.
LINTHORPE
Old English 'Leofing's hamlet' (or 'dependent farm').
LINTON
Old English 'farmstead amongst lime-trees' or 'in the flax'.
LINTZ
Under Norman French influence, the pronunciation of the Old English *hlinch*, 'hill', became *lints*. Its modern spelling is said locally to have been affected by the settlement of German sword-makers here.

LINTZGARTH

Related to *Lintz*, above. To the Old English *hlinch* has been added Middle English *garth*, originally meaning 'enclosed ground used as a paddock or garden', and subsequently meaning simply 'farm' - 'hillside farm'.

LIPWOOD

May be Old English 'wood on a steep slope'. If so, the first part of the name is related to Modern English *leap*.

LITTLETOWN

A modern name, apparently first used in 1613 - 'little town'. The hamlet had previously been called *South Pittington*.

LIVERTON

Although *-ton* is probably Old English 'farmstead', the precise meaning of *Liver-* is unknown. Nearby are the more recent settlements of LIVERTON MILL and LIVERTON MINES.

LOANEND

'The end of the lane'. A modern name.

LOFTUS

Old Norse *lopthus*, 'house with an upper floor'. The place was so-named because houses with two storeys were very uncommon and worth remarking upon.

LONGFRAMLINGTON

See *Framlington*, above.

LONGHIRST

Old English 'long wooded hill'.

LONGNEWTON

See *Newton*, below.

LONGOVICIUM

See *LANCHESTER*, above, and *The Romans and Place-Names* in the Digest.

LONGWITTON

See *Witton*, below.

LORBOTTLE

Old English 'Leofhere's dwelling'. The second part of the name - which relates to modern Lowland Scots *bothy* - is also found in *Walbottle*, *Shilbottle*, *Newbottle* and *Budle*; see elsewhere.

LOW *(River)*

Started life as ancient British 'pool left (in the sand) by the receding tide'. The word is related to Gaelic *loch*, 'lake, sea arm'. Over time, its dialect meaning changed to 'tidal stream'.

LOW FELL

Self-explanatory; 'low fell'. *Fell* comes to us from Old Norse.

LOWICK

Old English 'dairy farm on the river Low'. For *Low*, see above.

LOW LYNN

A dialect form of Old English 'waterfall on the river Low'. For *Low*, see above.

LUCKER

Old Norse 'sandpiper marsh' or perhaps 'palm-shaped marsh' - 'palm' here is the palm of a hand. The second part of the name - *ker* - is also found in *Byker* and *Walker*; see elsewhere.

LUDWORTH

Old English 'Luda's enclosed farmstead'.

LUMLEY

Early written forms of the name - *Lummalea, Lummelei, Lummesleie, Lumeleia* - suggest a meaning of 'clearing by the pool', although 'lamb clearing' has been suggested.

LUNE *(River)*

Like many river names, this is of ancient Celtic origin and probably means 'health-giving'.

LUTTERINGTON

Probably Old English 'Lothere's farmstead'.

LYHAM

Old English 'homestead by a clearing'.

LYNE *(River)*

An ancient Celtic river-name, perhaps meaning 'flowing'.

LYNESACK

This unusual name is probably Old English 'Leofwine's oak (tree)' - possibly a boundary marker tree.

MAIDEN LAW

Although *Law* is Old English *hlaw*, 'hill', I can find no explanation for *Maiden*.

MAINSFORTH

Seems to be Old English 'Maegen's ford' (across the little River Skerne).

MALTBY

Old Norse 'Malti's farm'.

MARDEN

May be Old English 'boundary valley'.

MARDON

Old English 'boundary hill'.

MARLEY HILL

Marley is Old English 'clearing at the boundary'. *Hill* is a later Viking addition.

MARSDEN

Seems to be Old English 'marsh valley', although, geographically, this is unlikely or at least puzzling.

MARSKE BY THE SEA

A Scandinavianised form of Old English 'the marshes'. *By The Sea* was added in Victorian times to make the town sound more attractive as a seaside resort. Nearby is the more recent settlement of NEW MARSKE.

MARTON
Usually Old English 'farmstead by a lake' though 'by a boundary' is also possible.

MASON
First recorded as *Merdisfen* in 1242, this is Old English 'Maerheard's fen'.

MATFEN
Old English 'Matta's fen'.

MEADOWFIELD
A modern name for the pit village which developed here. It seems to be a farmer's field name.

MEDOMSLEY
Appears to be derived from Old English *medumest-leah*, 'middlemost clearing'.

MELDON
Old English 'hill with a monument (or cross) on the top'.

MELKRIDGE
Old English 'milk ridge'. Presumably, cattle that grazed here were very productive.

MERRINGTON, KIRK
Merrington is Old English 'farmstead of Maera's people'. *Kirk,* 'church', is a later, Scandinavian, addition - the hilltop church here is indeed the settlement's most striking feature.

MERRYBENT
Seems to be Old English 'bentgrass field at the boundary'.

METAL BRIDGE
A Victorian name for the hamlet which, for indeterminate reasons, grew up around the bridge carrying the East Coast main line over the old Coxhoe to Spennymoor road.

MICKLETON
Old English 'large farmstead'.

MICKLEY
Old English 'large clearing'.

MIDDLEHAM, BISHOP
Middleham is Old English 'middle homestead'. *Bishop* was added when the Bishops of Durham established a favourite castle here.

MIDDLESBROUGH
Old English *midleste burg,* 'middlemost fortified place, fortified place in the middle'.

MIDDLESTONE
Early written forms of this name are confusing, although it is thought that the first element may be descended from an ancient Celtic word meaning 'bare hill' - 'stone on a bare hill'. At the foot of the hill, on what must have been heathery open land, lies MIDDLESTONE MOOR, now virtually part of Spennymoor.

MIDDLETON
Old English 'middle farmstead'. The name is so common that it is usual for a distinctive addition to be made:

> LITTLE MIDDLETON was the name given in the 19th century to the scattered settlement built between the old and new docks at Hartlepool.
> MIDDLETON IN TEESDALE is 'in Teesdale';
> MIDDLETON ONE ROW had only one row of cottages;
> MIDDLETON ST GEORGE from the dedication of the church.

MIDDRIDGE
Old English 'middle ridge'.

MIGLEY
Old English 'clearing infested with midges'.

MILLFIELD
Old English 'outlying land by the mill'.

MILTON
Old English 'farmstead with a mill'.

MINDRUM
This name originates in Old Welsh, and relates exactly to *Mynydd Drymmau* in Glamorgan; 'mountain with a ridge'.

MINSTERACRES
The presence of a monastery here is coincidental. The name is Middle English 'millstone acres'; that is, fields where stone suitable for millstones was found.

MITFORD
Old English 'ford at a confluence (where two streams meet)'.

MOLESDON
Old English 'Mol's farmstead'.

MONKSEATON
Old English 'farmstead by the sea owned by monks' - *monks-sea-ton*. The monks were those of Tynemouth. Nearby is WEST MONKSEATON.

MONKTON
Old and Middle English 'monks' farmstead' - the manor belonged to the monks of Jarrow from the 11th century.

MOORSHOLM
Old English 'at the houses on the moor'; there are three, including GREAT and LITTLE MOORSHOLM.

MOORSLEY
Probably Old English 'clearing on the moor'. Local people divide this small settlement into LOW and HIGH MOORSLEY.

MORDON
Old English 'hill on the moor'.

MORLEY
Old English 'clearing on the moor'.

Morpeth, Northumberland

MORPETH
Recorded in 1200 as *Morthpath*, this is Old English 'murder path'. Unfortunately, we will never know the nature of the horrific crime that took place hereabouts.

MORTON
Old English *mor-tun*, 'farmstead on the moor'.

       MORTON PALMS was held by Bryan Palmes until 1569;

       MORTON TINMOUTH belonged to Tynemouth Priory.

MORWICK
Old English 'dairy farm in a fen'.

MOUSEN
Old English 'Mul's fen'.

MUGGLESWICK
Old English 'Mucel's dairy farm'.

MURTON
Means the same as *Morton*, above - 'farmstead on the moor'.

NAFFERTON
Old Norse 'Nattfari's farmstead'. *Nattfari* was a nickname meaning 'night traveller'.

NEASHAM
The first part of the name is from the Middle English word for 'nose'; Neasham is 'homestead by the nose-shaped bend (of the River Tees)'.

NELSON
A colliery village named by the coal-owner in honour of Admiral Lord Nelson, victor of the Battle of Trafalgar in 1805.

NESBIT and NESBITT

A puzzling name with at least three possible interpretations. Firstly, a *nesebit* is 'the iron that passes across the nose of a horse and joins the branks together'; was the place named from some perceived similarity between it and this item of horseware? Or is the name descended from Middle English *nese-byht*, 'nose-shaped bend'? The third possibility derives the name from Old English 'Nes's bend'.

NETHERTON

Old English 'lower farmstead'.

NETHERWITTON

See *Witton*, below.

NETTLESWORTH

There are two closely related possibilities here, both from Old English. The name may mean either 'Nithbeald's farmstead enclosure' or '(at) Aethel's farmstead enclosure'.

NEVILLE'S CROSS

Although there was a pilgrim's cross here beforehand, the settlement seems to take its name from a replacement cross erected by Sir Ralph Neville in thanks for victory at the Battle of Neville's Cross in 1346.

NEWBIGGIN

A Middle English name derived from Old Norse; it means 'new dwelling'. As either *Newbiggin* or *Newbegin*, this name is oddly common in the North-East. There are at least two in County Durham, two in North Yorkshire and four in Northumberland (including NEWBIGGIN BY THE SEA).

NEWBOTTLE

Old English 'new house (cottage, dwelling)'. The second part - also to be found in *Walbottle*, see below - is related to modern *bothy*.

NEWBROUGH

Old English 'new fort'.

NEWBURN

Seems to be Old English 'new fort (or castle)'.

NEWCASTLE UPON TYNE

This is the settlement's third name. It started life as the Roman camp of *PONS AELIUS*, 'Hadrian's Bridge'; *Aelius* was the family name of the Emperor Hadrian. After the Roman departure, the camp fell into disuse and decay until its discovery by Saxon settlers, who established a small abbey here and called it *MONKCHESTER*, 'Roman fort of the monks'. The settlement became strategically important after the Norman Conquest; in the 12th and 13th centuries, a 'new castle' was built here and gave us the name we use now. See also *Tyne*, below.

NEWFIELD

A farmer's field name - 'field newly taken into cultivation'.

NEWHAM

Old English 'new homestead'.

NEWMINSTER

Middle English 'new minster'. The minster - a Cistercian Abbey - was founded in 1137; only small parts of it survive.

NEWSHAM

Old English '(at the) new houses'.

NEWTON

This is Old English 'new farmstead', and is a particularly common name; there are dozens all over England. Local Newtons include:

> NEWTON BY THE SEA, from its site and divided into LOW and HIGH;
>
> NEWTON CAP The *cap* here may refer to the hill above which the settlement lies.
>
> NEWTON ON THE MOOR, from its site;
>
> NEWTON UNDER ROSEBERRY, also known as *Newton in Cleveland*; its suffixes are obviously derived from its position. For *Roseberry Topping* and *Cleveland*, see above and below.
>
> NEWTON UNDERWOOD - 'beneath a wood';
>
> KIRKNEWTON - 'with a church';
>
> LONGNEWTON, from the shape of the settlement;
>
> WESTNEWTON, 'west of Newton'.

In mediaeval and modern times, *Newton* was also occasionally added to the name of an older settlement in order to name a newer one established nearby. See *Aycliffe* and *Bewley* above.

NEWTOWN

Middle English 'new hamlet'. The name is fairly modern.

NEW YORK

Originally a farm, and named - for some reason - in honour of the settlement of the American city.

NINEBANKS

Middle English 'nine banks'. The banks are by the River *Allen*; see above.

NO PLACE

This uniquely eccentric name seems to have originated as a miner's nickname for the pit here; it was 'no place' to work!

NORHAM

Middle English 'north homestead'. The original, Saxon name of the settlement was *UBBANFORD*, 'Ubba's ford'.

NORMANBY

Old Norse 'farm of the Northmen, or Norwegians'.

NORTHUMBERLAND

As originally used by Saxon settlers in the region, this name referred to all of present-day England 'north of the Humber', as well as to some parts of lowland Scotland. Over time, the northernmost parts of *Northhymbralond* were ceded to Scotland, and the western and southern parts gained names of their own (*Cumberland*, 'land of the ancient Britons'; *Westmorland*, 'land of the people who live west of the moors'; *Yorkshire*, 'shire centred around York'). By about 1065, it seems to have meant present-day Northumberland and County Durham. The latter became a County Palatine after the Norman Conquest, and from the 12th century onwards, *Northumberland* referred to the approximate area it covers now.

NORTON

Old English 'north farmstead' (a farmstead north of another). It is a very common name all over England.

NUNNYKIRK

Middle English 'nuns' church'.

NUNTHORPE

Old English 'farm of the nuns'. There was a nunnery here in mediaeval times.

NUNWICK

Old English 'nun's dairy farm'.

OAKENSHAW

Derived from Old English *acen-scaga*, 'oak wood'. *Shaw* has, of course, survived into modern English as a rarely-used word for a wood or copse.

OFFERTON

The exact meaning of this name is unclear; it may be Old English 'farmstead above the ford' (over the River Wear) - *up-ford-ton*.

OGLE

This sonorous name is - prosaically - Old English 'Ocga's hill'.

ONCE BREWED

This was the name of a wayside inn here. Presumably, it describes the nature of the beer. Nearby TWICE BREWED may be an early example of oneupmanship.

ORD

Old English 'sword, point'. The settlement is divided into EAST and SOUTH ORD. Perhaps the nearby sharp ridge is being referred to here; MIDDLE ORD lies at its top.

ORMESBY

Old Norse 'Orm's farm'. Nearby is NORTH ORMESBY.

ORNSBY HILL

Old Norse 'Ormr's farm'.

Otterburn, Northumberland

OTTERBURN
Old English 'otter burn'. Nearby is the modern army base of OTTERBURN
CAMP.

OUSE BURN
There are two possibilities here. The name may derive from a supposed Old
English name *Geose*, 'gushing' (the initial sound survives in the related name
Jesmond - see above). Or it may be very much older, derived from an ancient
Celtic word meaning 'surging, bubbling'. *Burn* is a later Viking addition.

OUSTERLEY
Early forms of the name indicate that it may be derived from an Old English word
for 'house-tree', though no-one seems to know exactly what a house-tree was.

OUSTON (County Durham, and Northumberland, near Stamfordham)
Old and Middle English 'Ulfkell's farmstead'. *Ulfkell* is an Old Danish name.

OUSTON (Northumberland, near Whitfield)
Old English 'Ulf's (or Wulf's) farmstead'.

OUTCHESTER
Old English 'Roman fort inhabited by owls'. The original, Roman, name for the
fort here is unknown.

OVINGHAM

Old English 'homestead of Ofa's people'. The name is pronounced *ovinjm*.

OVINGTON (Cleveland)

Old English 'farmstead of Wulfa's people'.

OVINGTON (Northumberland)

Old English 'farmstead of Ofa's people'. Ovington is near *Ovingham*, above; the same Ofa must have been involved with both.

OWTON

Appears in the charters of Finchale Priory as *Oveton*; it is probably Old English 'Ofa's farmstead'.

OXENHALL

Hall is, here, a corruption of Old English *healh*, 'corner, nook'. The name thus means 'ox nook, sheltered place for oxen'. The place is now called *OXEN LE FIELDS*, which is really *Oxenhall le Fields* - 'in the fields'.

OXFORD

Old English 'ford used for oxen'. The much more famous Oxford means the same thing.

OXHILL

Self-explanatory 'ox hill'. The name is Middle English.

PAGE BANK

I can find no explanation for this name.

PAINSHAW

Means the same as *PENSHAW*; see below.

PALLINSBURN

Seems to be Old English 'stream of Paelloc's people'.

PALLION

First occurs as *le Pavylion* in 1328. It is the Old French word *pavillon*, which has survived into Modern English as *pavilion*. Its mediaeval meaning suggests a structure - not necessarily temporary - built for a special purpose, and belonging to a larger building or institution. Perhaps Pallion was the site of a retreat or rest home for the monks of Wearmouth and Jarrow.

PASTON

Old English 'Palloc's farmstead'. The name is pronounced - and often spelt - *Pawston*.

PAUPERHAUGH

This striking name was *Papwirthhaugh* in 1100; it is apparently Old English 'water-meadow (*haugh*) belonging to someone from Papworth'. *Papworth* is 'Papa's farmstead enclosure', though it is unclear whether Papworth - an important Saxon estate in modern Cambridgeshire - is being referred to here.

PEGSWOOD

Old English 'Pecg's farmstead enclosure'.

PELAW

(pronounced *pee-law*) Probably Old English 'Paelli's barrow (burial mound)'. The Pelaw near Chester le Street may well be named after the same Paelli who gave his name to nearby *Pelton* - see below.

PELTON

Old English 'Paelli's farmstead'. This may be the same Paelli who is commemorated at nearby *Pelaw* - see above. Near Pelton there is also WEST PELTON and PELTON FELL; *fell* is used here to mean a low (rather than a high, Lakeland-type) moor.

PENNINES, THE

Over-enthusiastic antiquarian Charles Bartram (1723-1765) claimed to have found a mediaeval manuscript which mentioned *Pennines* as the name of the range of hills that straddles central Northern England from Derbyshire to the Scottish border. The manuscript was, however, a forgery by him. So we must credit the ingenious Mr Bartram with inventing this hauntingly ancient-sounding name. No-one knows where he got the name from or what inspired him; until his time, there was no single name for the whole chain of hills, which were - and still are - given local names instead.

PENNYWELL

I can find no explanation for this charming name.

PENSHAW

Seems to be derived from two Old Celtic words; *pen*, 'head, top', and *cerr* (or *carr*), 'rocks' - 'at the top of the rocks'. The *sh* sound would, in that case, be present under later Norman French influence. Support for this ancient derivation may well come from the almost mystical significance attributed to Penshaw Hill by the custom and folklore of local people.

The more northerly settlement of *PAINSHAW* has the same derivation.

PERCY MAIN

The name of a colliery that worked the High Main seam of coal north of the Tyne. The coal owner was honouring the ancient family name of the Dukes of Northumberland.

PERKINSVILLE

Named from *Perkins* and Partners, one-time owners of Birtley and Ouston collieries, who built the settlement.

PETERLEE

Arose from nothing as a New Town in 1948. At the instigation of the engineer and surveyor of Easington Council, it was named after Peter Lee (1864 - 1935), the mining union leader and lay preacher, who was born in nearby Trimdon Grange, and who spent most of his life there as a miner and administrator.

PHILADELPHIA

Of course the world-famous name of a great American city; it is derived from Greek for *brotherly love*. As elsewhere - see *Modern Names* in the Digest - the coal-owner applied it here to glorify his enterprise.

PHOENIX ROW

This old mining village consists of only one terrace of houses, whose name this is.

PICKTREE

Individual trees often occur in place-names, usually as boundary markers - see *Lynesack, Leasingthorne, Hawthorn*. This one seems to be Old English 'Pice's tree' (*Pice* is modern 'pike') though it may also mean 'tree rich in resin'. See also *Fir Tree*, above.

PIERCEBRIDGE

Early written forms of this name are confusing. It may mean 'Percy's (or Piers') bridge'. It is more likely, however, to be related to Old English *persh*, 'osier willow' - 'bridge by the osiers'. The name of the Roman fort here may have been *MORBIUM*, of unknown origin and meaning.

PIGDON

Old English 'Pica's pasture' or 'peaked hill'.

PITTINGTON

Old English 'hill of Pita's people'. Local people differentiate between LOW and HIGH PITTINGTON, as well as PITTINGTON HALLGARTH - see *Hallgarth* above.

PITY ME

There has naturally been much speculation about the meaning of this most extraordinary place-name. Amongst the theories proposed is that it derives from French *petite mer*, 'little sea', that it refers to a pitted, uneven meadow (a 'pitty mea') or that it may be a corruption of ancient British words for 'field of graves'. These explanations are, however, unsatisfactory at best, and the meaning of the name remains stubbornly and frustratingly unknown.

PLASHETTS

From the name of the Norman landowner here; *de Plessis*. This Old French surname was adapted from *Plaissiet* in France; the name means 'fenced-off area; parkland'.

PLAWSWORTH

Interestingly, the first part of this name is derived from Old English *plega*, 'play games', so *Plawsworth* may well be 'the farmstead enclosure (*worth*) for sports and games', proving that our distant ancestors did such things! Alternatively, early forms of the name suggest that the 'farmstead enclosure' may have belonged to someone with a name like *Plegmund* - 'the playful one'!

PLENMELLER

An ancient British name. *Plen-* relates directly to Modern Welsh *blaen,* 'top', found in *Blaen*au Ffestiniog. *-Meller* relates to Welsh *Moelfre*, ' bare hill'. Thus, 'top of the bare hill'. Nearby is the bare hilltop of PLENMELLER MOOR.

PLESSEY
Derives from the same Norman French source as *Plashetts*, above.

PONS AELIUS
See *NEWCASTLE UPON TYNE*, above, and *The Romans and Place-Names* in the Digest.

PONT *(River)*
An Old Celtic word, related to Welsh *pant*, 'valley'. See also *Pontop*, below.

PONTELAND
The name is Old English and means either 'island in the River Pont' or 'land by the River Pont'. The name is pronounced with stress on the second syllable; *PontEland*. For *Pont*, see above.

PONTOP
A complex name. *Pont* is the name of the burn which flows through the valley here - it is Old Welsh 'valley'; see *Pont* above. Anglo-Saxon settlers, ignorant of the meaning of *Pont*, added *hop*, 'valley' - *Pont-hop*, 'valley of the Pont'. *Pontop* is thus tautological; 'valley valley'. The highly visible hilltop nearby is known as *Pontop Pike*.

PORT CLARENCE
The port and transshipment terminus of the Clarence Railway. This eastward extension of the Tees and Weardale Railway, built in 1827, was named in honour of the Duke of Clarence, the future King William IV.

PORTGATE
The settlement lies at a gateway in the Roman Wall and its old Latin name was at first preserved - *port*, 'gate'. Later Saxon settlers added their own word *geat*, 'gate'. The name thus means 'gate gate'.

PORTOBELLO
This modern name commemorates the capture of Portobello, Panama, by Admiral Vernon in 1739.

POWBURN
This name is a combination of Old Welsh 'slow-moving' and Old English 'stream'.

PRENDWICK
Old English 'Praen's dairy farm'.

PRESSEN
Recorded as *Prestfen* in 1177, this is Old English 'priest's fen'.

PRESTON
A common place-name everywhere; it is Old English *preosta-tun*, 'farmstead of the priest'. There are at least four, including:

> PRESTON GRANGE A *grange* was a kind of mediaeval outlying farm dependent upon another, larger one.
> PRESTON LE SKERNE The distinguishing addition here is self-explanatory, but see also *Skerne*;

81

PRESTON ON TEES   The distinguishing addition here is also self-explanatory, but see also *Tees*

PRESTWICK
Old English 'priest's dairy farm'.

PRUDHOE
Old English 'Pruda's hillspur'.

QUAKINGHOUSES
I can find no explanation for this highly unusual name.

QUARRINGTON HILL
Early forms of this name are confusing. It may be derived from Old English *cweorn*, 'mill' - 'hill at the mill farmstead'. The presence of so many quarries hereabouts is probably coincidental. Nearby is the older settlement of OLD QUARRINGTON.

QUEBEC
This name commemorates General Wolfe's victory at the Battle of Quebec in 1757.

RABY
Old English (from Old Norse) 'village at a boundary'. It is not known which boundary is referred to. The village was swept away when the parkland of Raby Castle was laid out.

RAINTON
Recorded as *Reiningtone* in 1170, the name could easily have become *Rennington* (as indeed it did further north in Northumberland - see below). It is Old English 'farmstead of Regna's people'. There are five Raintons - EAST, MIDDLE, WEST, RAINTON BRIDGE and RAINTON GATE. This last has Old Norse *gata*, 'road'.

RAMSHAW
Old English 'raven's wood'. *Raven* may here have been someone's name, or nickname.

RAMSHOPE
Seems to be Old English 'valley where wild garlic grows'.

RATCHWOOD
Old English 'outlaw's wood'. The first part of the name is derived from *wraecca*, 'outlaw, fugitive', Modern English 'wretch'. It is seen again at *Wrekendike*; see below.

RAVENSWORTH
Old English 'Hraefn's farmstead enclosure'. The personal name *Hraefn* means 'raven'.

REAVELEY
Old English 'rough clearing'.

REDCAR
A hybrid name combining Old English *hreod*, 'reed', with Old Norse *kiarr*, 'marsh': 'reedy marsh'.

82

REDE *(River)*
Old English 'the red one'. The river's valley is REDESDALE.
REDMARSHALL
Rodmerehil in 1208; it is Old English 'hill by a reedy lake' (reed-mere-hill).
RED ROW
A modern name, from the colour of the original row's roofs.
REDWORTH
Old English 'farmstead enclosure where reeds grow'.
RENNINGTON
Old English 'farmstead of Regna's people'. The name is a version of *Rainton*, above.
RICKLETON
Rykelingden in the 14th century. It is Old English 'Ricela's farmstead'.
RIDING MILL
Modern 'the mill near Riding'. RIDING is Old English 'area cleared for cultivation'; that is, 'ridded' of trees and stones. There is also NUNRIDING - 'the part of Riding belonging to nuns'.
RIDLEY
Old English 'cleared grove'. There is also NEW RIDLEY.
RIDSDALE
Old Norse 'valley of the reddish stream'.
RIPLINGTON
Old English 'farmstead of the Riplingas'. *Riplingas* has been translated as 'dwellers by the strip of land'.
RISEBRIDGE
Middle English 'bridge made of brushwood'. The meaning intended is surely 'causeway'.
RISINGHAM
Old English 'homestead of Hrisa's people'; it is pronounced *rise-injm*. The Roman fort here was called *HABITANCUM*; although the meaning of this name is unclear, it may be '(fort built on) land belonging to Habitus'.
RITTON
Old English 'farmstead on a stream'.
ROBEY
Means the same as *Raby*, above - 'village at a boundary'.
ROCHESTER
Old English 'Roman fort inhabited by rooks'. The Roman name for their settlement here was *BREMENIUM*, 'by the roaring stream'.
ROCK
Unsurprisingly, Old English 'rock'.

RODDAM
Old English 'at the clearings'.
ROKEBY
Old Norse 'Hroca's farm', or 'farm where rooks were plentiful'.
ROKER
Earliest written forms of this name make its meaning very uncertain; it may be Old English 'Hroc's marsh'. *Hroc* was a personal name meaning 'rook'.
ROMALDKIRK
Old Norse 'St Rumwald's church'.
ROOKHOPE
Old English 'rook valley'. The name is pronounced *roo-kup*.
ROSEBERRY TOPPING
This rather pleasing name for the highest point of the Cleveland Hills is not an easy one to trace. *Roseberry* is first recorded as late as the 12th century as *Othenesberg*. It seems to be Old Norse 'Othin's hill'. The transition from the old name to the new may stretch our imagination; however, *-berg* would have been pronounced *-berry*, and the intrusive initial *R* may be a carry-over from a preceding preposition *undeR*. I have been unable to determine when the word *Topping* was added to the name of this hill.
ROSEDEN
Old English 'valley where rushes grow'.
ROSEWORTH
Seems to be Old English 'farmstead enclosure of (or near) rushes'.
ROSS
An ancient Celtic name relating to Modern Welsh *rhos*, 'headland, promontory'.
ROTHBURY
Old English 'Hrotha's fortified place'.
ROTHLEY
Old English 'grove with a clearing'. Nearby is the larger, more recent settlement of ROTHLEY MILL.
ROWLEY
Old English 'rough clearing'.
ROYAL OAK
Takes its name from the 19th century inn which once stood at the crossroads here.
RUDCHESTER
Old English 'Roman fort belonging to Rudda'. The original, Latin name of the fort here was *VINDOBALA*, which has been translated as 'white peak' or 'bright peak'.
RUGLEY
Old English 'woodcock clearing'.
RUMBY HILL
Old Norse 'hill at Hromundr's farm'.

RUNNING WATERS

This low-lying hamlet's name seems to have originated as a fairly recent farmer's field-name for a particularly boggy part of his farm which may also, perhaps, have been prone to winter flooding.

RUSHYFORD

Seems to be Middle English 'rushy ford, ford where rushes grow'.

RYAL

Old English 'rye hill' - the same as *Ryle*, below.

RYHOPE

Reofhoppa in 1050; it is Old English 'rough (or rugged) valley'.

RYLE

Old English 'rye hill' - the same as *Ryal*, above. The settlement is sometimes known as *GREAT RYLE*.

RYTON

Old English 'rye farmstead'.

SACRISTON

Until the pit village developed in modern times, the geographical name here was *Sacristonheugh* - recorded as *Segrysteynhogh* in 1312 - meaning 'spur of land (*heugh*) belonging to the sacristan'. The *sacristan*, or sacrist, was 'the keeper of sacred things' at - in this case - Durham Cathedral. The word - which has survived into Modern English as *sexton* - started life from Old French *segrestein*, a fact commemorated in the local pronunciation of the name: *Seggison* or *Seggiston*.

SADBERGE

Old Norse *setberg*, 'flat-topped hill'. *Setberg* is a fairly common place-name in Norway and Iceland.

ST JOHN'S CHAPEL

Takes its name from the chapel which existed here in 1335. The present chapel was built in 1752.

SALTBURN BY THE SEA

Saltburn is - perhaps unsurprisingly - Old English 'salty stream'. *By The Sea* was added in the late 19th century to increase the town's attractiveness as a seaside resort.

SALTER'S GATE

A Viking name; 'the salter's road'. There are several historical references to salt being won hereabouts, and this was the road used by the salt supplier - the *salter* - to reach his market to the east.

SANDHOE

Old English 'sandy hill spur'.

SANDYFORD

Old English 'sandy ford'.

SATLEY

Seems to be Old English 'camp clearing, clearing used for camping'.

SCARGILL
Old Norse 'narrow valley of mergansers'.

SCOTS GAP
Commemorates a fabled battle between local people and Scottish 'reivers' (livestock thieves) that took place at a 'gap' or secret entrance to the night-fold where the animals were being kept before being driven north.

SCOTSWOOD
Richard, son of John Scot, enclosed the West Wood of Benwell here in 1367.

SCRAINWOOD
Basically, Old English *screawena wudu*, 'wood of shrews'. *Shrew*, though, had the alternate meaning of 'rascal, villain'; this could be 'rascal's wood' as well!

SCREMERSTON
A Norman French family name is concealed within this Saxon-looking place-name; *Escrimeur*, descended from Old French for 'fencer'. This is 'Escrimeur's hamlet'.

SEABURN
Seems to be Old English 'burn near the sea'.

SEAHAM
Unsurprisingly 'homestead by the sea'. The name is Old English. Nearby SEAHAM HARBOUR is an entirely 19th century settlement, founded by coal magnate Lord Londonderry in 1828.

SEAHOUSES
A modern name; 'houses by the sea'.

SEAL SANDS
Self-explanatory. Although seals hereabouts are now an understandable rarity, they are still commonly seen off the nearby sea-coast.

SEATON
Old English 'farmstead by the sea'. There are several, including NORTH SEATON and:

> SEATON CAREW immortalises one Petrus *Carou*, who once held the manor here;
>
> SEATON BURN from the small stream on which it stands, the *Seaton Burn* - the 'burn that flows into the sea at Seaton';
>
> SEATON DELAVAL was held by the *de la Val* family, whose name comes from *le Val* in Normandy;
>
> SEATON SLUICE To make a small floating harbour here - and a new, shorter, outlet to the sea - Lord Delaval carved a 900ft canal in a deep cutting and erected within it a 'sluice', or movable watergate, in the 1760s

See also *MONKSEATON*, above.

SEDGEFIELD
May mean either 'Cedd's (or Secg's) pastureland'. *Secg* is Old English 'warrior', used here as a personal name.

86

SEGEDUNUM

See *WALLSEND*, below, and *The Romans and Place-Names* in the Digest.

SEGHILL

The derivation of this name is still a matter of some conjecture. The first element is thought to be the old name of the stream here; *Sige*, an Old English name meaning 'sluggish, slow-moving'. Or this could have been the nickname of the settler here. The second part of the name means 'nook', not 'hill'.

SELABY

Seems to be a hybrid name combining Old Norse 'village' with Old English 'willows' - 'village by the willow copse'.

SETTLING STONES

The name dates back at least to the 13th century, and seems to refer to 'saddling stones'. These would be the large boulders used by travellers to remount their horses - to 'saddle' - after the climb up Grindon Hill. For *Grindon*, see above.

SEWINGSHIELDS

Old English 'Sigewine's shelters'.

SHADFORTH

Old English 'shallow ford'. The name of the little stream here - the *Shald* - appears to be a back-formation from *Shad*forth (rather than the other way round).

SHAFTOE

Old English 'hillspur with a shaft (or pole)'. The structure would probably have been a boundary marker or meeting place.

SHARPERTON

Old English 'farmstead by the steep hill'. The hill is now called SHARPERTON EDGE.

SHARPLEY

Old English 'clearing on a steep hill'.

SHAWDON

Old English 'valley by a wood'.

SHERATON

The meaning of this name is uncertain; it may be Old English 'Scurfa's farmstead'.

SHERBURN

Old English *scir-burna*, 'bright (clear, pure) stream'. *Scir* was 'Scandinavianised' by later Viking settlers as the name of the River Skerne - see below. Local usage denotes the original ancient settlement as *SHERBURN VILLAGE* and the nearby pit village as *SHERBURN HILL* (from the escarpment on which it was built). *SHERBURN HOSPITAL*, founded in 1181, is about a mile away, and is also regarded locally as a separate settlement.

SHIELDFIELD

Old English 'open land with huts on it'.

The Market Place, South Shields.

SHIELDS, NORTH, SOUTH and HIGH

Derived from Old English *scheles*, 'huts, shelters', often used by fisherfolk (as at North and South Shields, which are separated by the River Tyne).

The Roman fort at South Shields - extensive remains of which can still be seen - was called (in Latin) *ARBEIA*. Although its meaning is unknown, the native Celtic people have retained it; the Modern Welsh name for South Shields is *Urfa*, a corruption of *Arbeia*.

SHILBOTTLE

Seems to be 'dwelling of the Shipley people'. There is a Shipley not far away; see below.

SHILDON

Old English 'shelf-shaped hill'.

SHILVINGTON

Old English 'farmstead of the dwellers on a shelf'. *Shelf* is, here, a shelf-shaped piece of land.

SHINCLIFFE

Contains Old English *scinna*, 'spectre, demon, ghost' and seems to mean 'haunted cliff'. Supernatural or pagan/heathen references of this sort are rare - and tantalising - in place-names; County Durham has another at *Harrowgate* - see above.

SHINEY ROW

Shiney is derived from Old English 'beautiful'. *Row* was often used to denote a patch of countryside. Thus 'beautiful country'.

SHIPLEY

Old English 'sheep clearing, pasture for sheep'.

SHIREMOOR

Middle English 'shire fen' - the fen marking the boundary of the old shire of Tynemouth.

88

SHITLINGTON
May be Old English 'farmstead of Scytta's people'.
SHITTLEHOPE
Seems to be Old English 'valley of Scytla's people'.
SHORESTON
The (sea)shore is not involved here. The name is derived from Old English 'Sceot's farmstead'. *Sceot* seems to have been a nickname meaning 'quick'.
SHORESWORTH
Old English 'farmstead enclosure on a steep slope'.
SHORTFLATT
Seems to be Old English 'short furlong'.
SHOTLEY
Old English 'clearing of the Scots'.
>   SHOTLEY BRIDGE is, of course, 'the bridge to Shotley'.
>   SHOTLEY FIELD is the 'outlying pasture near Shotley'.
SHOTTON (Northumberland)
Old English 'hill of the Scots'. There are two, including SHOTTON IN GLENDALE. See *Glen*, above.
SHOTTON (near Peterlee)
Probably Old English 'farmstead of the Scots'.
>   OLD SHOTTON is now part of Peterlee, and also gave its name to nearby SHOTTON COLLIERY.
SHOTTON (near Stockton)
Old English 'farmstead on a slope'.
SILKSWORTH
Although the first part may be a reference to silk in some way or other, it seems more likely that the name is Old English 'Seolc's farmstead enclosure'.
SIMONBURN
Old English 'Sigemund's stream'.
SIMONSIDE (Northumberland)
Old English 'Sigemund's land'.
SIMONSIDE (South Shields)
Old English 'Sigemund's fold'. *Fold* here is 'place where animals are kept' - as in 'sheepfold'.
SINDERHOPE
Probably Old English 'Sindri's valley', though the name could also indicate 'southern valley'.
SKELTON
Started life as Old English *Sceltun*, 'farmstead on a shelf-shaped hill'. and would normally have become *Shelton* or *Shilton*. Later Viking settlers, however, applied their own pronunciation to the name. There are several, including, SKELTON

GREEN, grazing land for the use of the people of Skelton, and NEW SKELTON. Some local people also regard SKELTON CASTLE as a separate village.

SKERNE *(River)*

This name is probably from Old English *scir*, 'bright, clear' - the same word occurs in *Sherburn* (see above), except that, under later Scandinavian influence, we have *sk* instead of *sh*.

SKINNINGROVE

Old Norse 'the skinner's pit'. It is a rare reference to the place where a craftsman essential to Viking life - the skinner of domestic and wild animals - lived and worked.

SLAGGYFORD

This evocative name has an equally evocative meaning; it is Old English 'muddy, dirty ford'.

SLALEY

Old English 'muddy clearing'.

SLEEKBURN

Old English 'muddy stream'.

SLINGLEY

First recorded in 1155 as *Slingelaw*; it contains Old English *sling*, 'noose, loop, snare', and means 'hill where animals were snared'.

SMALES

The earliest name here was that of the stream, which was called the *Smale*, from Old English *smael*, 'narrow'. Beside it were the settlements of *Smales*, 'of the Smale', and *SMALESMOUTH*, '(at the) mouth of the Smale'. A degree of 'back-formation' then occurred; the stream was thought to take its name from the settlements (rather than the other way round) and became the *SMALES BURN*, which it still is.

SNITTER

Although this name may derive from Middle English words meaning 'snow' or 'icy blast', its meaning remains a mystery.

SNODS EDGE

Middle English 'hill ridge near The Snods'. THE SNODS is Old English 'snowy places'.

SOCKBURN

First recorded as *Soccabyrig* as early as 780; two quite different interpretations have been put on the name. It may mean - prosaically - 'Soca's fortified place' (*byrig* is 'fortified place') or - more exotically - 'fortified place of the Soke'. A *soke* was a sort of Anglo-Saxon judicial inquiry or inquisition and, although Sockburn is known to have been an important pre-Conquest religious site, its exact meaning here is unknown.

SOFTLEY
Old English 'soft clearing'. *Soft* here means 'spongy', and presumably refers to the soil.

SOUTH BANK
A modern name, the *South Bank* of the Tees. The settlement developed in late Victorian times.

SOUTH MOOR
Unsurprisingly 'moor to the south (of, presumably, Stanley)'.

SOUTH TONGUES
Late Middle English 'tongues (of land) to the south'.

SOUTHWICK
Old English 'south dairy farm'.

SPENNYMOOR
The precise meaning of *spen* is unknown. *Spennymoor* may, though, mean 'hedged moor, moor with hedged enclosures'. See also *High Spen*, above.

SPINDLESTON
Apparently Old English 'spindle rock'; presumably, a stone that looked like a spindle.

SPITAL TONGUES
This unforgettable name seems to refer to tongues of dry land in nearby marshy ground, that belonged to a hostel or hospital, often an institution caring for travellers as well as the sick.

SPITTAL and SPITTLE
Old English 'hostel, inn, hospital'. See *Spital Tongues*, above.

SPRING GARDENS
Seems to take its name from the small terrace of industrial houses built here to service the railway. There was an important junction and crossing at this point.

SPRINGWELL
Probably Old English 'spring by a copse'.

STAINDROP
Conventionally, Staindrop is derived from Anglo-Saxon *staen-thorp*, 'stoney village'. Other suggestions, however, include 'stoney valley' (from *staener-hop*) and 'Stegen's village' (*Stegen-thorp*). Early written forms are confusing and any of these meanings is possible, though the first still seems the most likely.

STAINMORE
Probably Old English 'stoney moor'.

STAINSBY
Old Norse 'Stein's farm'. The site of the deserted mediaeval village now lies under the A19 road.

STAINTON and NUNSTAINTON
Stainton is a Scandinavianised form of Old English *stan-tun*, 'stoney farmstead'. The *Nun* prefix is here because the manor was once held by a convent.

STAINTON, GREAT and LITTLE (north of Darlington)

Although this Stainton may mean the same as the ones above, early written forms of the name - *Staninctuns, Steningtun* - suggest a more likely derivation from *stanweg-tun* 'farmstead by a paved (Roman) road'; Great Stainton sits astride an ancient Roman crossroads.

STAMFORD

Old English 'stoney ford'.

STAMFORDHAM

Old English 'homestead at the stoney ford'. See *Stamford*, above.

STANEGATE

Old English 'stone (paved) road'. The Saxons gave this name to the road that ran behind Hadrian's Wall and connected up the forts along its length.

STANGHOW

Old Norse 'hill with a pole'. The pole was probably a boundary marker.

STANHOPE

Old English *staen-hop*, 'stoney valley'. It is pronounced *stannup*.

STANLEY

Old English *staenig-leah*, 'stoney clearing'. 'Officially', the smaller of the two places with this name is called STANLEY CROOK - 'near Crook'.

STANNINGTON

Old English 'farmstead on the paved road'. The road in question is the Great North Road.

STANTON

Old English 'farmstead on stoney ground'.

STAPLE ISLAND

One of the Farne Islands, this takes its name from Old English *stapol*, 'pillar, post' - apparently from the pillars of rock which characterise it. For *FARNE ISLANDS*, see above.

STARTFORTH

Old English *straet-ford*, 'ford on a Roman Road'.

STATION TOWN

The 19th century colliery development of Wingate (for which, see below).

STAWARD

Old English *stan-worth*, 'farmstead enclosure made of stone'.

STEEL

Old English 'steep hill'.

STELLA

Stelyngleye in 1183. It is Old English 'clearing with a stelling'. A *stelling* was a cattle-fold, a place provided for cattle to shelter from the sun.

STELLING

Old English 'cattle shelter, stall'.

STILLINGTON
Old English 'farmstead of Styfel's people'.

STOBSWOOD
Old English 'wood by a tree-stump'. The first part of this name is also found in *Elstob*, above.

STOCKLEY
Place-names with *stock* or *stoke* are amongst the most difficult to define clearly. This is because they may be derived from either one of two Old English words, both of which changed their meanings in ancient times - *stoc*, which started life meaning simply 'place' (but which developed several other meanings, like 'monastic cell'), and *stocc*, which meant 'tree stump or log'. So *Stockley* may mean either 'clearing linked to another place' or 'stockaded clearing'.

STOCKSFIELD
Old English 'pastureland linked to another place' or 'stockaded pastureland'. For problems associated with *Stock-* names, see *Stockley*, above.

STOCKTON ON TEES
May mean either 'farmstead dependent on another place' or 'stockaded farmstead' - see *Stockley*, above.

STOTFOLD
Old English 'stud-fold'.

STRANTON
Old English 'farmstead on the strand (on the shore)'.

STREATLAM
Old English *Stretleam*, '(at the) clearing by the Roman road'.

STREETGATE
May be an unusual combination of Old English 'Roman road' (*street*) with Old Norse 'road' (*gate*); thus 'road to the Roman road'.

STURTON GRANGE
Sturton is apparently Old English 'farmstead on a Roman road'. The meaning is uncertain; no Roman road is known to have passed by here. *Grange* was often used of an outlying tenanted farm supplying goods and materials to a larger one.

STYFORD
Old English 'path over a ford'.

SUGLEY
Old English 'sparrow clearing'.

SUMMERHOUSE
Middle English 'house used in summer'.

SUNDERLAND (Tyne and Wear)
Old English *sundorland*, 'separate land'. The meaning may be simply 'private land', or 'land separate from the main estate'. The 'original' Sunderland occupied the small corner of land on the south bank at the mouth of the River Wear. It may have been land 'sundered from', but still owned by, the monastery of

Monkwearmouth over the river, or perhaps it was the only land *not* owned by the Church - and thus 'private'.

SUNDERLAND BRIDGE

The bridge here - still standing - is 13th century. It is unclear, however, whether the nearby settlement took its name from the bridge, or whether *Bridge* was added to the pre-existing name of the settlement, with the same meaning as *Sunderland* above ('separate land') with the purpose of differentiating the two.

SUNDERLAND, NORTH

Oddly, this name means 'southern land to the north'. *North* was added, of course, to differentiate this settlement from the larger - and growing - Sunderland to the south; see *Sunderland (Tyne and Wear)*.

SUNNISIDE

Early written forms of the name are rare. It may mean 'Sunnan's place'. Sunbathing is certainly not involved.

SUNNYBROW

Although I can find no early records of this name, it may be Middle English 'Sunnan's hill'.

SWAINSTON

Old English 'Swegen's farmstead'.

SWALWELL

Old English 'swallow spring, spring where swallows flock'.

SWARLAND

Old English 'heavy land', that is, land heavy to plough.

SWEETHOPE

Apparently Old English 'sweet (pleasant) valley'.

SWINBURN, GREAT

Old English 'pig brook'.

SWINHOE

Old English 'pig hill'.

SWINHOPE

Old English 'swine valley'.

TANFIELD

First recorded as *Tamefeld* in 1179; it seems to be Old English 'field by the River Team' - see *Team*, below.

TANTOBIE

I can find no explanation for this sonorous name, which is pronounced with stress on the second syllable. Local information has suggested a derivation from *Team-hop-by*, 'farm in the valley of the Team'. If this is correct, the name is an unusual combination of Old British (*Team*), Old English (*hop*) and Old Norse (*by*).

TARSET

May be Old English 'Tir's (animal) fold'.

TEAM *(River)*

Like many local river- and stream-names, *Team* is descended from an ancient Celtic word, here said to mean 'dark'. The same word has given us the rivers *Thames*, *Tamar*, *Thame*, *Tame* and *Teme*. The industrial and residential development on the east flank of the river, below Gateshead, is known as TEAMS.

TEES *(River)*

The meaning of this name is uncertain, although it has been suggested that - like many local river names - it is of ancient British (Celtic) origin, and may mean 'boiling, surging'.

> *TEESDALE* is conventionally used for the western upper reaches of the river and *TEESSIDE* for the conurbation around Stockton and Middlesbrough.

THICKLEY

Old English 'thick (dense) wood'.

THINFORD

Although *-ford* seems to be Old English 'ford', I can find no explanation for *Thin-*

THIRLWALL

Old English 'punctured wall'. There must have been a gap in Hadrian's Wall here.

THIRSTON

Old English 'Thraesfrith's farmstead'. The settlement is divided into EAST and WEST.

THOCKRINGTON

Seems to be Old English 'farmstead of the Unsteady One' - a nickname whose significance we may only guess at.

THORNABY

Old Norse 'Thormoth's farm'.

THORNBROUGH

Old English 'fortified place where thorns grow'.

THORNGRAFTON

Old English 'farmstead by a thorn-brake'.

THORNLEY (near Wheatley Hill)

Old English 'thorney hill, hill with thorn trees'.

THORNLEY (near Wolsingham)

Old English 'thorney clearing, clearing amongst thorn trees'.

THORNTON

Old English 'farmstead where thorn-trees grow'. There are at least four, including EAST and WEST THORNTON.

THORPE

Old English *throp*, the precise meaning of which is uncertain. It may have meant 'dependent farm', 'hamlet' or 'village'. Local people refer to this settlement as *LITTLE THORPE*. There are two others:

> THORPE BULMER belonged to Ralph de Bulmer in the 14th century.
>
> THORPE THEWLES Worryingly, *Thewles* is Old English 'immoral', and would have been pronounced *thew-less*.

THRISLINGTON

Old English 'Thorstein's farmstead'.

THROCKLEY

Probably 'Throca's hill', although the first element may also be descended from Old English *throc*, a complex word which originally meant 'a piece of timber on which the ploughshare is fixed', and came to mean 'trestle', 'table' and even 'prop'.

THROPHILL

Old English 'hill farm'.

THROPTON

May be Old English 'farmstead at a crossroads'.

THROSTON

Old English 'Thori's farmstead'.

TILL *(River)*

This is an ancient Celtic river-name whose precise meaning is unknown. It may relate to an Old Welsh word for 'flow' and mean 'stream'.

> At the river's mouth is TILMOUTH.

TIPALT BURN

Tipalt seems to be Old English *aet Yppewalde*, 'at the shelf wood'; that is, the wood on a plateau. This is the stream which runs by here.

TIPTOE

For many years, this charming name was thought to be derived from that of the 13th and 14th century Norman landowners here - *de Tipetot*. It is now suggested, however, that it was *they* who adapted the place-name as their own, and that the name originated as Old English *aet Yppehoh*, 'at the shelf spur'; that is, the spur of land at the edge of the plateau.

TITLINGTON

Old English 'farmstead of Titel's people'.

TODHILLS

A Middle English name, from Old Norse, this may mean either '(of) Todda's (or Tuda's) hill' or - more likely - 'fox holes'.

TODRIDGE

Middle English 'fox ridge'.

TOGSTONE

Old English 'Tocga's valley'.

TOFT HILL

Toft comes to us from Old Norse and, in English place-names, means 'site of a large house' or 'deserted site'. *Toft Hill* may therefore mean 'hill where there was a house'.

TOLLESBY

There are several possible explanations for this Old Norse name. It may be 'Toll's (or Toln's) farm', or 'the farm where the toll-gatherers (or tax collectors) lived', or 'the farm where tolls (or taxes) were paid'.

TONE

In 1296, this was *Tolland*. It may be Old English 'land on which a toll was paid'.

TORONTO

Commemorates the Canadian Campaign of 1757. For other 'imperial' names of this type, see *Modern Names* in the Digest.

TOSSON

May be derived from Old English *tot-stan*, 'look-out stone', though this is uncertain.

TOW LAW

First appears in 1423 as *Tollawe*. The exact meaning of the name is uncertain; it may be a corruption of Old English *tot hlaw*, 'look out hill' - which would certainly suit the town's exposed hilltop situation.

TRANWELL

Old English 'cranes' stream'.

TREWHITT

Old Norse 'low-lying meadow for dry wood'.

TREWICK

Old English 'dairy farm by a tree'.

TRIMDON

First recorded in 1196 as *Tremeldon*, this name may be derived from Old English *treo-mael-dun*, 'hill with a wooden monument (or wooden cross)'. As well as the original settlement, locally called TRIMDON VILLAGE, there is also TRIMDON GRANGE, a mining village which developed around a large farmhouse of that name, TRIMDON COLLIERY, another pit village, and TRIMDON STATION, which developed around the station opened here to serve the area. This last village is more commonly known by local people as DEAF HILL (although I cannot determine why).

TRITLINGTON

Old English 'farmstead of Tyrhtel's people'.

TROUGHEND

First recorded as *Trocquen* in 1242, the meaning of this name is unknown.

TUDHOE

Old English 'Tuda's hill spur'.

TUNSTALL

Old English *tun steall*, 'place of a farm'.

TURSDALE
Trellesden in 1150. It is Old English 'Thrall's valley'.
TWEED *(River)*
Like so many other river-names, this is an ancient Celtic word. It is thought to mean 'swelling, powerful'.
At the river's mouth in Berwick is TWEEDMOUTH.
TWICE BREWED
See *Once Brewed*, above.
TWIZEL and TWIZELL
Old English *twisla*, 'fork of a river' (where a river divides into two). The word is found in *Haltwhistle*, above.
TYNE *(River)*
The exact meaning of this regionally important name is unknown. It may signify simply 'river', and be derived ultimately from an ancient Celtic word meaning 'dissolve, flow'.
At its upper reaches, the river is formed from the *NORTH TYNE* and *SOUTH TYNE*, and each of these has its own 'dale'. *TYNESIDE* is the conurbation on both sides of the river between Newcastle/Gateshead and the sea at Tynemouth/South Shields. The 'metropolitan county' of *TYNE AND WEAR* was formed as a bureaucratic nicety in 1974 and abolished a few years later.
TYNEMOUTH
Although its meaning is obvious, this is a very old Saxon name; it was *Tinan muthe* in AD792.
ULGHAM
Old English 'owl corner'. The name is pronounced *uffm*.
ULNABY
May be Old Norse 'Ulfhethinn's farm'.
ULWHAM
This rather odd name means the same as *Ulgham*, above; 'owl corner'. The second element is found on its own at *Wham*, below.
UNTHANK
The origin of this name is uncertain; it may be a mediaeval farmer's field-name - 'ungrateful (stubborn, unproductive) field' - or, more likely, it may be related to Old English *unthances*, 'without leave', referring to a squatters farm.
UPLEATHAM
'On the upper slope'. The name started life as Old English *Leatham*, 'on a slope'. Later Viking settlers added *Up* to distinguish this settlement from *Kirkleatham* (see above) which lies below it.
URLAY NOOK
This sonorous name may be Old English 'nook by the bison clearing'.

URPETH
Old English 'bison path', perhaps referring to the native wild ox. Nearby are HIGH and LOW URPETH.
USHAW
Old English *wulf-scaga*, 'wolf wood'.
USWORTH
Old English 'Oca's farmstead enclosure'.
VERCOVICIUM
See *HOUSESTEADS* above, and *The Romans and Place-Names* in the Digest.
VIGO
This area of Birtley was developed in the early 18th century; its name commemorates the capture by the British of the Spanish seaport of Vigo in 1719.
VINDOBALA
See *RUDCHESTER*, above, and *The Romans and Place-Names* in the Digest.
VINDOLANDA
See *CHESTERHOLM*, above, and *The Romans and Place-Names* in the Digest.
VINDOMORA
See *EBCHESTER*, above, and *The Romans and Place-Names* in the Digest.
VINOVIA
See *BINCHESTER*, above, and *The Romans and Place-Names* in the Digest.
WACKERFIELD
The precise meaning of this name is uncertain. The first part may be derived from an Old English word for 'willow' (which has come into Modern English as *wicker*); 'willow-field'.
WALBOTTLE
Old English 'house (farm, cottage) on the (Roman) Wall'. Nearby is NORTH WALBOTTLE. The unusual *-bottle* ending can also be found at *Newbottle* and *Shilbottle*.
WALDRIDGE
Apparently Old English 'ridge with (or by) a wall'.
WALKER
Old Norse *walkiarr*, 'marsh by the (Roman) Wall'. Nearby is WALKERGATE, 'the road to Walker'.
WALL
Old English 'wall'. The settlement sits astride the Roman Wall.
WALLINGTON
Old English 'farmstead of Wealh's people'.
WALLISH WALLS
Middle English 'old building occupied by a Welshman'.
WALLSEND
Despite its obvious meaning - 'the end of the (Roman) Wall' - this name, like

Tynemouth above, is deceptively old; it is Saxon Old English *Wallesende*. The Roman name for their fort here was *SEGEDUNUM*, which may have meant 'victory fort' or 'strong fort'.

WALLTOWN
Middle English 'hamlet on the Roman Wall'.

WALWICK
Old English 'dairy farm on the Roman Wall'. The name is pronounced *wolick*.

WALWORTH
Old English 'farmstead enclosure of the foreigner'. Ironically, Anglo-Saxon settlers usually used the word *wealh*, 'foreigner', to mean a native Celtic Briton. There was obviously a settlement of native British Welsh-speakers here. This use of *wealh* has given us *Wales*, '(land of) the foreigners'.

WANDYLAW
Probably Old English 'windy hill'.

WANSBECK *(River)*
The exact derivation of this name is not known for certain. It is possible, though, that the river took its name from a bridge that once crossed it; the name may mean 'bridge that can be crossed by a wagon'.

WARDEN
Old English *weard-dun*, 'watch hill, look-out hill'. There are three: HIGH and NETHER ('lower') WARDEN and WARDEN LAW. *Hlaw*, 'hill' was added here when the meaning of *Warden* had been forgotten. The modern name thus means 'watch hill hill'.

WARDLEY
May be descended from the same word - *weard* - as *Warden*, above. If so, it means 'the watchman's clearing'.

WARK
Old English 'works, fortifications'.

WARKWORTH
Old English 'farmstead enclosure by the fortification works'.

WARREN BURN
An ancient British river-name, this means 'alder stream'.
> On the stream are WARENFORD (Old English 'ford over the Warren Burn') and WARENTON (Old English 'homestead on the Warren Burn').

WARRENBY
Although - *by* is Viking 'farm', I can find no explanation for the *Warren* part of this name.

WASHINGTON
Seems to be Old English 'farmstead of Waesa's people'.

WASKERLEY
Early forms of this name - *Wascroppe*, *Wascroppeheved* - are particularly

confusing. It may mean 'at the head of Wealaca's valley', or perhaps 'clearing at the watery marsh'.

WATERHOUSES

Unsurprisingly, 'houses by the water'.

WEAR *(River)*

Old English *Wior*, or *Weor*. This in turn is descended - like many river and stream names - from a native Celtic word which has also given us the River *Weser* (in Germany), and which is thought to mean simply 'water, river'.

> *WEARDALE* is conventionally used for the western upper reaches of the river, *WEARSIDE* for Sunderland and area, and *WEAR VALLEY* for the middle reaches of the river between Weardale and Durham City. The village of *WEARHEAD* lies at the point where the river is formed from the Killhope and Wellhope burns. The 'metropolitan county' of *TYNE AND WEAR* was formed as a bureaucratic nicety in 1974 and abolished a few years later.

WEARMOUTH

The area around the mouth of the River Wear. It is called BISHOPWEARMOUTH on the south side and MONKWEARMOUTH on the north. The areas belonged to the Bishop and monks of Durham respectively.

WEEDSLADE

Old English 'withy valley'.

WEETWOOD

Old English 'wet wood'.

WELDON

Old English 'valley with a stream'. The settlement is really WELDON BRIDGE.

WELTON

Old English 'farmstead by a spring'.

WESTERHOPE

Old English 'whetstone valley, valley where whetstones were quarried'.

WESTERTON

Old English 'western farmstead'.

WESTGATE

A fairly late name - it does not occur until the 15th century, when the Weardale hunting grounds of the Bishops of Durham were laid out and fenced. This was where the 'west gate' into the park stood. There is also *EASTGATE*.

WESTNEWTON

See *Newton*, above.

WESTOE

Seems to be Old English 'Wifurth's hill spur'.

WESTWICK

Old English 'western dairy farm'.

WHALTON
Old English 'farmstead at a rounded hill'.

WHAM
This unusual place-name is descended from Old English *hwamme*, 'corner'. (Where Old English spelt words with *hw*, Modern English often changes the letters round to *wh*, as in *hwaete*, 'wheat' and here at Wham.) The word is also found in *Ulwham*, above.

WHARMLEY
May be Old English 'clearing in a kettle-shaped valley'.

WHEATLEY HILL
Old English 'hill by a wheat clearing (a clearing used for growing wheat)'.

WHELPINGTON
Old English 'farmstead of Hwelp's people'. *Hwelp* was a nickname meaning - perhaps unsurprisingly - 'puppy'. There are two; KIRKWHELPINGTON ('with a church') and WEST WHELPINGTON.

WHESSOE
Seems to be Old English 'Hwessa's hill spur'. It may also mean 'steep hill spur', except that the hill here is not at all steep.

WHICKHAM
Two Old English meanings have been suggested for Whickham; 'homestead with a dairy farm' or 'homestead with a quickset hedge'.

THE VILLAGE GREEN, WHICKHAM.

102

WHITBURN
Probably Old English 'Hwitta's tumulus' or perhaps - less likely - 'Hwitta's burn'. (A *tumulus* is an artificial burial mound.) Nearby was once WHITBURN COLLIERY.

WHITCHESTER
Old English 'white Roman fort', presumably from the colour of the stones here. The original Roman name of the fort has been lost.

WHITEHILL
Unsurprisingly, Old English 'white hill'.

WHITFIELD
Old English 'white pastureland'.

WHITLEY BAY
The settlement here was originally *Whitley*, Old English 'white clearing'. *Whitley Bay* is really a geographical feature - 'the bay at Whitley'.

WHITTINGHAM
Old English 'homestead of Hwita's people'. Many local people pronounce the name *whitinjm*.

WHITTINGTON
Old English 'farmstead of Hwita's people'. There are two - GREAT and LITTLE.

WHITTLE
Old English 'white hill'.

WHITTON
Either 'Hwitta's farmstead' or 'white farmstead' (from the colour of the building materials used) - both Old English.

WHITTONSTALL
Old English 'homestead with a quickset hedge'.

WHITWELL
Either 'white spring' or 'Hwitta's spring' - both Old English.

WHITWHAM
Old English 'white corner'. The second part of the name occurs in *Ulwham*, above, and on its own in *Wham*, above.

WHITWORTH
Old English 'Hwitta's farmstead enclosure'.

WHORLTON (County Durham)
Old English 'farmstead by the mill stream'.

WHORLTON (Northumberland)
Old English 'farmstead by a round hill'.

WIDDRINGTON
Old English 'farmstead of Wuduhere's people'. Nearby is the 19th century settlement of WIDDRINGTON STATION.

WIDDYBANK FELL
Probably Old Norse 'fell (high moor) by a willow hill'.

WIDE OPEN
This peculiar name seems to have a rather unexotic explanation; Old English 'wide valley'.

WILLIMOTESWICK
This extravagant name is Middle English 'Guillemot's dairy farm'. *Guillemot* has the same force as Modern English 'Little Willy'.

WILLINGTON
Old English 'farmstead of Wifel's people'. Near the Tyneside Willington is the modern settlement of WILLINGTON QUAY.

WILTON
Old English 'farmstead amongst the willows'.

WINDLESTONE
The -*stone* ending is a misleading corruption of Old English *dun*, 'hill'; this is 'Waendel's hill'.

WINGATE and WINGATES
Old English *gate* here is used to mean 'a gap in the hills, a pass'; the name means 'gap where the wind blows through'.

WINLATON
Winloctune in 1085. It is Old English 'Winelac's farmstead'.

WINSTON
Old English 'Wine's farmstead'.

WISHAW
Middle English 'Wishart's wood'. *Wishart* is a Norman name: *Guiscard*, 'wise beard'.

WITHERWACK
The first part of this exotic name may come from one of several sources; Old Norse 'wooded', Old English 'wether' (sheep) or Old English 'willow'. The second part remains a mystery.

WITTON
A fairly common name throughout England. Unfortunately, the precise Old English derivation of the names is often - as here - uncertain. Amongst the possibilities are 'farmstead by a dairy', 'white farmstead', 'wide farmstead', 'Wite's farmstead' and - most likely - 'farmstead by a wood'. There are several:

> WITTON LE WEAR, named for its position by the River Wear - the insertion of *le* is a common Norman-influenced method of distinguishing an older, common place-name element;
> WITTON GILBERT is named after its mediaeval French landlord Gilbert de la Ley - local folk-memory recalls this fact by pronouncing the name as *Jilbert*;

WITTON PARK is a pit village laid out in part of the parkland of nearby Witton Castle;

LONGWITTON is named for the shape of the settlement;

NETHERWITTON is 'lower Witton'.

WOLSINGHAM
Old English 'homestead of Wulfsige's people'.

WOLVISTON
Old English 'Wulf's farmstead'.

WOODBURN
Old English 'stream in a wood'.

WOODEN
Old English 'valley of wolves'. The name is pronounced *woo-den*.

WOODHAM
Old English '(at the) wood'.

WOODHORN
Old English 'wooded point of land'.

WOOLER
Seems to be Old English 'bank of a stream'.

WOOLEY
Old English 'wolf clearing'.

WOOLSINGTON
Old English 'farmstead of Wulfsige's people'.

WOOPERTON
May be Old English 'valley by the temple hill' - a rare reference to a pagan site.

WREIGH BURN
This name tells an unsavoury story; it is Old English 'stream where felons were drowned'.

WREIGHILL
This name has obvious links to *Wreigh Burn*, above. It is Old English 'hill where felons were executed'.

WREKENDIKE
The name the Anglo-Saxons gave to the remains of part of the Roman road to South Shields. Intriguingly, the name seems to mean 'fugitive's ditch (or dyke)', derived from Old English *wraecca*, 'fugitive, criminal', which has come down to Modern English as *wretch*. By Wrekendike is WREKENTON - 'farmstead of the fugitives' or 'farmstead by the Wrekendike'.

WYCLIFFE
May be Old English *wiht cliffe*, 'cliff by a bend (of the river)'.

WYLAM
The exact meaning of this name remains a mystery. It may be Old English 'at the trap (or watermill, or some other contraption)'.

WYNYARD

Old Norse 'meadow enclosure'.

YARM

Old English 'at the dam', probably a device erected to catch fish.

YEARBY

Old Norse 'upper farm'.

YEAVERING

An ancient Celtic name thought to mean 'goat hill'. Nearby *Yeavering Bell* is a prominent - and, to some, bell-shaped - hill.

YETLINGTON

Old English 'farmstead of Geatela's people'.

**The School House, Yetlington
Near Rothbury, Northumberland**

THE PLACE-NAMES DIGEST

The origins and meanings of place-names are extraordinarily diverse. And this means that they can be divided and classified into all sorts of groups - for example, by how old they are:

> Celtic (*Consett, Yeavering*)
> Norman French (*Beamish, Darras*)
> Modern (*Peterlee, Vigo*).

Or by ending:

> -by (*Rumby, Raby*)
> -ford (*Warenford, Gainford*)
> -ham (*Norham, Seaham*)
> -ley (*Slaley, Thornley*)
> -ton (*Chilton, Preston*)
> -wick (*Goswick, Elwick*)
> -worth (*Ludworth, Killingworth*) and others.

Many place-names mention domestic or wild animals: *Cassop, Urpeth, Wooden*. Others mention crops and other plants: *Wheatley Hill, Eppleton, Allerdean*. And there is a substantial group of names which, despite much academic endeavour and research, remain obstinately unexplained. The most well-known of these is *Pity Me*.

For interest, information and entertainment you will find on the next few pages, lists of the region's place-names grouped according to elements they have in common.

PLACE-NAMES WHICH FEATURE DOMESTIC AND OTHER ANIMALS

All of these names mention domestic - and sometimes wild - animals, or structures built to house, shelter or - at *Kepier* and *Slingley,* for example - to catch them. Note the number of wild animals that are now locally rare (deer) or extinct (cranes, wildcats, wolves and even bison).

BEAL	bees	FINCHALE	finches
BEWICK	bees	FISHBURN	fish
BOLDRON	bulls	FOWBERRY	foals
BOULMER	bullocks	FOXTON	foxes
BURDON	cattle	GATESHEAD	goats
BYERS GREEN	cattle	GIBSIDE	sheep(fold)
CALLALY	calves	GOSFORTH	geese
CALLERTON	calves	GOSWICK	geese
CASSOP	wildcats	HAMSTERLEY	corn weevils
CATCLEUGH	wildcats	HARDWICK	sheep
CATTON	wildcats	HAREHOPE	hares
COCKLAW	wild birds	HART	stags
COCKLE	wild birds	HARTBURN	stags
CORNFORTH	cranes	HARTFORD	stags
CORNHILL	cranes	HARTINGTON	stags
CORNSAY	cranes	HARTLAW	stags
COUNDON	cattle	HARTLEY	stags
COWPEN BEWLEY	hen coops	HARTON	stags
COWSHILL	cattle	HARWOOD	hares
CRAMLINGTON	cranes	HAUXLEY	(poss) hawks
CRASTER	crows	HAWKHILL	hawks
CRAWCROOK	crows	HAWKWELL	hawks
CRAWLEYSIDE	crows	HEATHERSLAW	deer
CULLERCOATS	pigeons	HENDON	hinds
CUSHAT LAW	wood-pigeons	HINDLEY	hinds
DOLLAND	doves	HORSLEY	horses
EDMUNDBYERS	cattle	KELLOE	calves
ELTON	eels	KEPIER	fish
ELVET	swans	KYLOE	cattle
EMBLETON	caterpillars	KYO	cattle
EWESLEY	blackbirds	LAMBLEY	lambs
FAWDINGTON	animal fold		

LAMBTON	lambs	STELLING	cattle-fold
LAMESLEY	lambs	STOTFOLD	horses
LUCKER	sandpipers	SUGLEY	sparrows
LUMLEY	lambs	SWALWELL	swallows
MIGLEY	midges	SWINBURN	pigs
OTTERBURN	otters	SWINHOE	pigs
OUTCHESTER	owls	SWINHOPE	pigs
OXENHALL	oxen	TARSET	fold, shelter
OXFORD	oxen	TODHILLS	foxes
OXHILL	oxen	TODRIDGE	foxes
RAMSHAW	ravens	TRANWELL	cranes
ROCHESTER	rooks	ULGHAM	owls
ROKEBY	rooks	ULWHAM	owls
RUGLEY	woodcock	URLAY NOOK	bison
SCARGILL	mergansers	URPETH	bison, wild
SHIPLEY	sheep	USHAW	wolves
SIMONSIDE	sheepfold	WOODEN	wolves
SLINGLEY	game	WOOLEY	wolves
STELLA	cattle-fold	YEAVERING	goat-hill

PLACE-NAMES WITH -*BY*

The name ending -*by* comes ultimately from an Old Norse word used by the Vikings, but whose meaning is imprecise. It is perhaps safest to define it as 'farm', and this is what I have done in the Dictionary. Place-names with -*by* are rare in this region, where Viking penetration was superficial. There appears to be none at all in Northumberland, and those listed occur almost entirely in the south of the area. Against each name, I have given the meaning of its second element.

AISLABY	Aslakr's	ROBEY	at a boundary
COULBY	charcoal	ROKEBY	Hroca's, or rooks
GILMONBY	Gilman's	RUMBY HILL	Hromundr's
INGLEBY	English	SELABY	near willows
KILLERBY	Kilvert's	STAINSBY	Stein
LACKENBY	Lochan	TANTOBIE	in the valley of
LAZENBY	freedman		the River Team
MALTBY	Malti	THORNABY	Thormoth
NORMANBY	northmen	TOLLESBY	tax gatherer
ORMESBY	Orm	ULNABY	Ulna's
ORNSBY HILL	Ormr's	YEARBY	upper
RABY	at a boundary		

PLACE-NAMES FROM OLD BRITISH

The oldest inhabitants of these islands about whose language we have some knowledge were the Celts, who had settled here about three thousand years ago after a long migration from Asia Minor. Although most of their place-names have disappeared under succeeding migrations or invasions of Romans, Anglo-Saxons, Vikings and Normans, those listed here are thought to be of Old British (Old Welsh) origin, or to contain Celtic elements. They are our oldest place-names.

ALLEN	unknown	LYNE	flowing
ALN	unknown	LUNE	health-giving
ALWIN	unknown	MIDDLESTONE	bare hill
AYLE	unknown	MINDRUM	ridged mountain
BALDER	peak water	OUSE	surging, bubbling
BREAMISH	roaring ?	PAINSHAW/	
CAMBOIS	bay	PENSHAW	head of the rocks
CARRAW	rocks	PLENMELLER	top of the bare
CHEVIOT	unknown		hill
CHRISTON BANK	hill	PONT	valley
COCKER BECK,		PONTOP	valley
COCKERTON	crooked	POWBURN	slow-moving
CONSETT	hilltop	ROSS	headland
DEERNESS	river	TANFIELD	River Team
DERWENT	river, oak	TEAM	dark
DEVIL'S WATER	black stream	TEAMS	River Team
	(poss)	TEES	surging
DON	water	TILL	poss 'stream'
ERRING	bright as silver	TWEED	swelling,
FONT	unknown		powerful
GLEN	clean, holy	TYNE	flow
GLENDUE	dark valley	WARREN (BURN)	alder stream
KIELDER	violent stream	WEAR	water, river
KIRKLEY	hill	YEAVERING	goat hill
LACKENBY	Lochan		
LEVEN	smooth		
LOW	tidal pool		

PLACE-NAMES WITH -*CLIF*

Old English *clif* - the obvious ancestor of modern *cliff* - meant 'slope' or 'bank'; usually, though not necessarily, a steep one, and by no means always against the sea. Against each name - all Anglo-Saxon - I have given the meaning of its second element.

(SCHOOL) AYCLIFFE	by oak trees	HORNCLIFFE	in a tongue of
CLEADON	steep bank		land
CLIFTON	farmstead	SHINCLIFFE	haunted
CONISCLIFFE	the king's	WYCLIFFE	by a bend
EGGLESCLIFFE	Ecca, church		
HECKLEY	high, heathery		

PLACE-NAMES WHICH FEATURE COLOURS

Colours are mentioned in these place-names.

BLACK CALLERTON	black	FAWNLEES	multi-coloured, speckled
BLACKHALL	black		
BLACK HEDDON	black	FAWNS	multi-coloured
BLACKHILL	black	FAWSIDE	multi-coloured, speckled
BLACK MIDDENS	black		
BLACKWELL	black	GREENHAUGH	green
BLAGDON	black	GREENHEAD	green
BLAKELAW	black	GRINDON	green
BLANCHLAND	white	REDE	red
BLAYDON	black	RED ROW	red
BLEAKLAW	black	WHITCHESTER	white
BROWNEY	brown	WHITEHILL	white
BROWNIESIDE	brown	WHITFIELD	white
FALLOWDON	yellow	WHITLEY BAY	white
FALLOWFIELD	yellow	WHITTLE	white
FALSTONE	multi-coloured	WHITTON	white
FAWDON	multi-coloured	WHITWELL	white
		WHITWHAM	white

PLACE-NAMES FROM -*DENU*

These are all Anglo-Saxon names. Old English *denu* meant 'valley' - it is the origin of the modern word *dene*, much used locally. In the list below (which is not exhaustive), I have indicated by each name the meaning of its other elements.

ALLERDEAN	alder	EMBLETON	elms
AYDON	hay	FOXTON	foxes
BLAGDON	black	(HIGH) HANDENHOLD	Hana
CASTLE EDEN	God's	HENDON	hinds
CHIRDON	church/bendy stream	MARSDEN	marsh
DAWDON	near Dalton	SHAWDON	by a wood
DEBDON	deep	TOGSTONE	Tocga
DENWICK	dairy farm	WARDEN	look-out
DUDDOE	Dudda	WOODEN	wolves

PLACE-NAMES FROM - *DUN*

Old English *dun* meant 'hill' - it is the origin of the modern words *downs* (as in *South Downs)* and *dune*. All these place-names are Anglo-Saxon and incorporate *dun*; you will see that most - though not all - of them end with -*don*. I have indicated by each name the meaning of the other part(s) of the name.

AYDON	hay	HETTON	Heppe
BLAYDON	black	HOWDON	main, chief
BRANDON	broom	LANGDON BECK	long
(GREAT) BURDON	with a fortification	LANGTON	long
BUSTON	Buttel	MARDON	boundary
CALLERTON	calves	MELDON	monument
DOWNHAM	at the hills	SHILDON	shelf-shaped
FALLOWDON	yellow	WARDEN LAW	watch, look-
FLODDEN	by a stream ?		out
GRINDON	green	WINDLESTONE	Waendel's
HEDDON	heather		

PLACE-NAMES FROM -*FELD*

Old English *feld* differed in meaning from its modern descendant *field*. It was used by the Anglo-Saxons to refer to open land, land free from trees, or to outlying pasture land. Against each name, I have given the meaning of the other part(s) of the name.

ANNFIELD PLAIN	Ann's	FATFIELD	productive
BINGFIELD	Bynna	FLEMINGFIELD	John de
BITCHFIELD	beech		Flemyng
BOCKENFIELD	beech	MILLFIELD	with a mill
BROXFIELD	by a brook	SEDGEFIELD	Cedd's
BURNOPFIELD	in the river valley	SHIELDFIELD	with a hut
BUTSFIELD	Bota's, or by a	STOCKSFIELD	stockaded
	small piece of land	TANFIELD	by the River
CAWFIELDS	Cawa		Team
COCKFIELD	Cocca's	WACKERFIELD	near willows
FALLOWFIELD	yellow/newly-cultivated	WHITFIELD	white

PLACE-NAMES WITH - *FORD*

Old English *ford* meant precisely what it means now; a point where a river is shallow enough to wade across. Such points were vitally important to travel and trade in Saxon times; bridges were rare and often ruinous. Against each name, I have given the meaning of the other part(s) of the name.

ALLENSFORD	Aella's	HARTFORD	stags
ANNITSFORD	by a steep path	MAINSFORTH	Maegan's
BARRASFORD	by a grove	MITFORD	confluence
BELFORD	Bela?	OFFERTON	upper
BRADFORD	broad	OXFORD	oxen
CHOLLERFORD	Ceola/gorge	RUSHYFORD	where rushes grow
CORNFORTH	where there are cranes		
DEPTFORD	deep	SANDYFORD	sandy
DOXFORD	Docc	SHADFORTH	shallow
ELFORD	Ella/elder	SLAGGYFORD	muddy
FORD		STAMFORD	stoney
GAINFORD	direct, or Gaega's	STARTFORTH	on a Roman road
GOSFORTH	geese		
HARRATON	large	STYFORD	with a path
LINTZFORD	by the hill, or near Lint	WARENFORD	Warren Burn

113

PLACE-NAMES WITH -*HAM*

Old English *ham* - ancestor of modern *home* - could denote a range of settlement types to the Saxons, from 'village' to 'estate, manor' and 'homestead'. I have used the latter meaning in the Dictionary. Against each name, I have given the meaning of the other part(s) of the name. Place-names with -*ingham* are listed elsewhere.

ALNHAM	River Aln	LYHAM	by a clearing
BURGHAM	with a fort	(BISHOP) MIDDLEHAM	
FLEETHAM	by a stream		middle
GREATHAM	large, sandy	NEWHAM	new
HAMSTEELS	cattle shed, or steep bank	NEWSHAM	new
		NORHAM	northern
HARNHAM	cocky	STAMFORDHAM	at Stamford
HEXHAM	hagustald	WHICKHAM	with a dairy farm
HIGHAM	high		

PLACE-NAMES WITH -*HOH*

Old English *hoh* indicated a promontory of some kind; a high piece of land which ended abruptly, giving way to lower land or the sea. I have used 'hill-spur' in the Dictionary. The word survives locally as *heugh* ('*hyuff*'). With each of the names below - all Saxon - is the meaning of the other part(s) of the name.

CAMBO	crested	INGOE	Inga
CARLIN HOW	old hags, witches	KYO	cattle
CLAXHEUGH	Clacc	PRUDHOE	Pruda
COXHOE	Cocc	SANDHOE	sandy
DUDDO	Duddo	SHAFTOE	with a shaft
HEUGH	'hoh'	SWINHOE	pigs
HOUGHALL	nook	TUDHOE	Tudda
HOUGHTON	farmstead	WESTOE	Wifurth
		WHESSOE	Hwessa

PLACE-NAMES WITH -*HAUGH*

Saxon Old English *haugh* - a word still sometimes used locally - denoted a low-lying, fertile water-meadow, usually on the floor of a flat, wide valley. With each name in the list below is the meaning of the other part(s) of the name.

ANGRYHAUGH	used for grazing	HAUGHTON	farmstead
BRAINSHAUGH	with a burial mound	HEPPLE	hips
BROOMHAUGH	covered with broom	HOWTEL	wooded
ELYHAUGH	alders	HUMSHAUGH	Hun
FAIRHAUGH	pleasant	KIRKHAUGH	with a
GREENHAUGH	green		church
HAREHAUGH	old fort	PAUPERHAUGH	Papworth

PLACE-NAMES WITH -*HOP*

Although there is some variation, it is generally safe to assume that Old English *hop* was used by the Saxons to mean 'valley', particularly a 'blind' valley - one that is closed off at one end. As this list shows, these names usually, but not always, end in -*hope*. Against each name, I have given the meaning of the other part(s) of the name.

BLENKINSOPP	Blenkin	LINHOPE	lime-trees or flax
BOLLIHOPE	Bol's	RAMSHOPE	wild garlic
BROOMHOPE	broom	ROOKHOPE	where there are
BURNHOPE	with a stream		rooks
BURNOPFIELD	with a stream	RYHOPE	rough
CASSOP	with wildcats, or Casa's	SHITTLEHOPE	Scytla
		STANHOPE	stoney
HAREHOPE	hares	SWEETHOPE	pleasant
HEDLEYHOPE	of Hedley, or at the heathery clearing	SWINHOPE	with pigs
		TANTOBIE	of the River Team
HOPPEN	at the valleys	WESTERHOPE	whetstones
IRESHOPEBURN	of the Irish	WIDE OPEN	'at the wide...'
KILLHOPE	narrow		

PLACE-NAMES WITH -*INGHAM*

Place-names ending in -*ingham* denote that the settlement 'belongs' to a named settler and his/her people; it is their 'homestead'. These names all originated in Anglo-Saxon Old English; those marked * are usually pronounced -*injm*, an unexplained dialectal peculiarity of such names in Northumberland. Against each name, I have given the name of the settler(s).

BARNINGHAM	Beorn	ELLINGHAM*	Ella
BELLINGHAM*	hill dwellers	ELTRINGHAM*	Aelfhere
BELTINGHAM*	Belthor	OVINGHAM*	Ofa
BILLINGHAM	Bill	RISINGHAM*	Hrisa
CHILLINGHAM	Ceofel	WHITTINGHAM*	Hwita
EDLINGHAM*	Eadwul	WOLSINGHAM	Wulfsige
EGLINGHAM*	Ecwulf		

PLACE-NAMES WITH -*INGTON*

Place-names ending in -*ington* denote that the settlement 'belongs', usually to a named settler and his/her people; it is their 'farmstead'. These names all originated in Anglo-Saxon Old English. Against each name, I have given the name of the settler(s). The list is not exhaustive.

ACKLINGTON	Eadlac	(KIRK) MERRINGTON	Maera
BEDLINGTON	Bedla	OVINGTON	Wulfa
CARTINGTON	Certa	OVINGTON	Ofa
CHOPPINGTON	Ceabba	PITTINGTON	Pita
DARLINGTON	Deornoth	SHITLINGTON	Scytta
DINNINGTON	hill-dwellers	STILLINGTON	Styfel
DODDINGTON	Dudda	TITLINGTON	Titel
EASINGTON	Esi	TRITLINGTON	Tyrhtel
EDINGTON	Ida	WALLINGTON	Waesa
ESLINGTON	Esl	WHELPINGTON	Hwelp
FELKINGTON	Feoluca	WHITTINGTON	Hwita
HEIGHINGTON	Heca	WIDDRINGTON	Wuduhere
HEMLINGTON	Hymel	WILLINGTON	Wifel
LARTINGTON	Lyrti	WOOLSINGTON	Wulfsige
(KIRK)LEVINGTON	Leofa	YETLINGTON	Geatala
LUTTERINGTON	Lothere		

PLACE-NAMES WITH *-LEAH*

The original Anglo-Saxon meaning of Old English *leah* was 'an open place in a wood, part of a wood where the trees were scattered or cleared so that grass could grow'. It later came to signify a glade or grove. I have used the definition 'clearing' in the Dictionary. Most - but not quite all - names from *leah* end with *-ley*. The other parts of the names may refer to a named owner, crops grown in the clearing, impediments cleared away, to the clearing's site or position, or to some other identifying factor. Against each name in the list below (which is not exhaustive), I have given the meaning of the other part(s) of the name.

APPERLEY	apples	LEAMSIDE	at...
AYCLIFFE	oaks	LEE HALL	stone house
BEANLEY	beans	LUMLEY	lambs
BIRTLEY	bright	MARLEY HILL	boundary
BRADLEY	broad, wide	MEDOMSLEY	in the middle
CALLALY	calves	MICKLEY	large
CHEVELEY	Cifa	MOORSLEY	on a moor
COLLIERLEY	charcoal-burner	MORLEY	moor
DUDLEY	Dudda	OUSTERLEY	'house-tree'
ESPERLEY	east	REAVLEY	rough
ETHERLEY	Aethred's	RIDLEY	cleared
EWESLEY	blackbirds	ROWLEY	rough
FALLOWLEES	newly-cultivated	RUGLEY	woodcock
FARNLEY	ferns	SATLEY	for camping
FORTHERLEY	sheep-herders	SHIPLEY	sheep
FROSTERLEY	forester	SHOTLEY	scots
HAMSTERLEY	corn-weevil	SLALEY	muddy
HARPERLEY	harper	STANLEY	stoney
HARTLEY	stags	STELLA	cattle-fold
HEALEY(FIELD)	high	STOCKLEY	stockaded
HEALEY	high	STREATLAM	Roman road
HEDGELEY	Hidda	SUGLEY	sparrows
HEDLEY	heather	THORNLEY	thorn trees
HORSLEY	horses	URLAY NOOK	bison
HUNTERLEY	huntsman	WARDLEY	watchman
KNITSLEY	knight	WHARMLEY	kettle-shaped valley
IVESLEY	Ivo	WHEATLEY HILL	wheat
LAMBLEY	lambs	WHITLEY BAY	white
LANGLEY	long	WOOLEY	wolves

MODERN PLACE-NAMES

Modern place-names are generally regarded as those given since about 1400. North East England has a surprisingly large number of these, mostly because of the village- and town-building associated with industrial activity.

BEDLINGTON STATION	station
CHEVINGTON DRIFT	drift mine
CO-OPERATIVE VILLAS	workers' co-operative?
DORMANSTOWN	Dorman Long
DRAGONVILLE	George and Dragon pub
FENCEHOUSES	houses by a fence
FERRYHILL STATION	station
FOREST HALL	house of the forester
GRANGETOWN	town by the grange
GRANGE VILLA	Pelton Grange
GRAYTHORP	Sir William Gray
HAMILTON ROW	row of houses
KITTY BREWSTER	alehouse
LIVERTON MILL/MINES	from nearby Liverton
LOANEND	lane end
MEADOWFIELD	field-name
METAL BRIDGE	metal bridge
NEWFIELD	field-name
NEWTON AYCLIFFE	'new town'
NO PLACE	'no place' to work
PENNINES	invented; meaning not known
PERCY MAIN	stretch of High Main coal seam
PERKINSVILLE	Perkins and Partners
PETERLEE	Peter Lee
PHOENIX ROW	terrace
PORT CLARENCE	Duke of Clarence
RED ROW	roof colour
ROYAL OAK	pub
SEAHAM HARBOUR	'harbour'
SEAHOUSES	sea houses
SEATON SLUICE	sluice, watergate
SOUTH BANK	...of River Tees
SPRING GARDENS	terrace
STATION TOWN	station

| WIDDRINGTON STATION | station |
| WILLINGTON QUAY | quay |

To these can be added the many *Colliery* names, as well as those with *New*. A special group of Modern Names are those given by coal-owners or other industrial magnates to commemorate 'great moments in British imperial history'.

BLUCHER	General at Battle of Waterloo
HEIGHTS OF ALMA	Crimean War battle
INKERMAN	Crimean War battle
NELSON	Admiral Lord Nelson
NEW YORK	American city
PHILADELPHIA	American city
PORTOBELLO	City in Panama, captured in 1739
QUEBEC	Canadian campaign of 1757
TORONTO	Canadian campaign of 1757
VIGO	Spanish port, captured in 1719

PLACE-NAMES WHICH FEATURE *OCCUPATIONS*

These names mention the occupations of the settlers who lived there. Except for *Sacriston* (which is Old French) they are Old English.

BAGRAW	hawkers	MONKTON	monk
BICKERTON	bee-keeper	NUNSTAINTON	nuns
CARLTON	peasant	NUNTHORPE	nun
COLLIERLEY	charcoal-burner	NUNWICK	nun
COULBY	charcoal-burner	PRESSEN	priest
COWDEN	charcoal-burner	PRESTON	priest
FORTHERLEY	sheep-herder	PRESTWICK	priest
HARBOTTLE	hired worker	SACRISTON	sexton, sacristan
HARPERLEY	harper	SALTER'S GATE	salt-seller
HUNTERLEY	hunter	SKINNINGROVE	skinner
LESBURY	physician, doctor	TOLLESBY	toll gatherer
MONKSEATON	monk	WARDLEY	watchman

PLACE-NAMES FROM OLD FRENCH

Most places had already been named by the time of the Norman Conquest in 1066, and generally the Normans were content to retain pre-existing place-names. Where they built new settlements, though, the Normans gave them names in their native Old French. All of these names originated in this way.

BEAMISH	beautiful mansion	DARRAS (HALL)	d'Araynis
BEARPARK	beautiful retreat	DEVIL'S WATER	d'Eiville (poss)
BEAUFRONT	beautiful brow		
BELASIS	beautiful site	FLASS	pool, bog
BELLASIS	beautiful site	FOREST	forest
BELLISTER	fine place	FROSTERLEY	forester
BELMONT	beautiful hill	GUYZANCE	Guines
BEWLEY	beautiful place	HAGGERSTON	Hagard
BLANCHLAND	white launde	JESMOND	Ousemouth
BULBECK	Bolbec (family name)	PALLION	pavilion
		PLASHETTS	de Plessis
BUTTERBY	beautiful find	SACRISTON	sacrist
CAUSEY	embankment, raised way	SCREMERSTON	fencer
		WISHAW	Guiscard

Additionally, it became the occasional fashion to attach the name of a landowner or overlord to a pre-existing place-name, as at

COATHAM MUNDEVILLE	from	Thomas de Amundeville
DALTON PIERCY	from	Percy family
HURWORTH BRYAN	from	Brian, son of the Earl of Richmond
HUTTON HENRY	from	Henry de Essh
MORTON PALMS	from	Bryan Palmes
SEATON CAREW	from	Petrus Carou
SEATON DELAVAL	from	de la Val
THORPE BULMER	from	Ralph de Bulmer
WITTON GILBERT	from	Gilbert de la Laye

HUTTON MAGNA also has a Norman French suffix.

PLACE-NAMES WHICH FEATURE
CROPS AND OTHER PLANTS

All of these names mention farmed crops or other plants in one connexion or another.

ACKLAM	oak	HAYDON	hay
AKELD	oak	HEADLAM	heather
ALLERDEAN	alder	HECKLEY	(poss) heathery
ASHINGTON	ash	HEDDON	heather
AXWELL	oak	HEPPLE	hips
AYDON	hay	HESLEDEN	hazel
BARMOOR	cranberries	HOLEYN/HOLLIN	holly
BARWICK	barley	HULNE	holly
BEANLEY	beans	HYLTON	wild tansy
BENFIELDSIDE	bentgrass	ILDERTON	elder
BERWICK	corn	LEVER	iris, rush
BIRKENSIDE	birch	LINHOPE	lime or flax
BITCHBURN	beech	LINSHEELS	lime
BRANDON	broom	LINTON	lime or flax
BRECKON HILL	bracken	LYNESACK	oak
BRIERTON	briars	MERRYBENT	bentgrass
BROOM	broom	OAKENSHAW	oak
BROOMHAUGH	broom	PIERCEBRIDGE	osier willow
BROOMLEY	broom	RAMSHOPE	wild garlic
BROOMY HOLM	broom	REDCAR	reeds
CAISTRON	thorns	REDMARSHALL	reeds
CLAREWOOD	clover	REDWORTH	reeds
CLEATLAM	burdock	ROSEWORTH	rushes
CRESSWELL	watercress	RUSHYFORD	rushes
DERWENT	oak	RYAL	rye
EACHWICK	oak	RYLE	rye
ELFORD	elder	SELABY	willow
ELRINGTON	alder	THORNBROUGH	thorns
ELYHAUGH	alders	THORNGRAFTON	thorns
EPPLETON	apples	THORNLEY	thorns
ESH	ash	THORNTON	thorns
ESHOTT	ash	WEEDSLADE	withies, willow
FARNE	ferns	WHEATLEY HILL	wheat
FRANHAM	thorns	WIDDYBANK FELL	willow
HASWELL	hazel	WILTON	willow

PLACE-NAMES WITH -*WICK*

Old English/Old Norse *wic* has a complex history. It started life as an early Anglo-Saxon word borrowed from Latin *vicus*, 'a civil settlement'. Its adopted meaning changed fairly rapidly, through 'dwelling-place, village, hamlet, town' to 'farm'. Its specialist meaning in Viking lands was 'harbour, haven' - it gave the Vikings their name; 'harbour people'. By the 10th century, it had a more general force for Vikings; it had become 'a source of supplies' and so (as with Old English) a farm, particularly a dairy farm. This is the meaning I give it in the Dictionary, although it is not always possible to be precise. Generally, the other part(s) of the place-name may refer to a named owner of the *wic*, to its siting or position, or to a product obtainable there.

ABBERWICK	Aluburg	HOLWICK	in a hollow/
ALNWICK	River Aln		in holly
BARWICK	barley	HOWICK	high
BERWICK	corn	HUNWICK	Huna
BEWICK	bees	KEEPWICK	trading
BROTHERWICK	Brodor	LOWICK	River Low
BUTTERWICK	butter	MORWICK	in a fen
CHESWICK	cheese	MUGGLESWICK	Mucel
DENWICK	in a valley	NUNWICK	nuns
EACHWICK	by oak trees	PRENDWICK	Praen
ELSWICK	Aelfsige	PRESTWICK	priest
ELWICK	Aella	SOUTHWICK	to the south
FENWICK	by a fen	TREWICK	by a tree
GOSWICK	geese	WALWICK	on the Roman Wall
HARDWICK	sheep	WESTWICK	to the west
HAWICK	high	WILLIMOTESWICK	Guillemot

PLACE-NAMES WITH - *WORTH*

It is difficult to be precise about the meaning given by the Anglo-Saxons to Old English *worth*, although 'fenced homestead, farmstead enclosure' seems to be generally accepted. Usually, the other part(s) of the place-name refer to a named owner of the *worth*. They may also, however, indicate its siting, its use or its composition

ALDWORTH	old	PEGSWOOD	Pecg
BACKWORTH	Bacca	PLAWSWORTH	playing games,
CLAREWOOD	clover		or Plegmund
EWART	river	RAVENSWORTH	Hraefn
HEDWORTH	on the heath	REDWORTH	reeds
HEWORTH	high	ROSEWORTH	rushes
HUNSTANWORTH	Hunstan	SHORESWORTH	steep slope
HURWORTH	enclosed with	SILKSWORTH	Seolc
	hurdles	STAWARD	made of stone
KIBBLESWORTH	Cybbel	USWORTH	Oca
KILLINGWORTH	Cylla	WALWORTH	foreigner
KIMBLESWORTH	Cynehelm	WARKWORTH	by a fortification
LUDWORTH	Luda	WHITWORTH	Hwitta
NETTLESWORTH	Nithbeald,		
	or Aethel		

PLACE-NAMES WHICH FEATURE NATIONALITY AND RACE

When the Saxons and Vikings migrated to these shores, they did not, of course, arrive in an empty land. Native Celtic people had already been here for a thousand years and had seen the Romans come and go, and pockets of them remained in the area long after the latest migrants settled. The Saxons and Vikings sometimes ironically called them 'foreign' (*wealh*, as in *Walworth*, and modern *Welsh*). As this list shows, other nationalities drifted around here too.

FLEMINGFIELD	Flemish (Belgian)	SHOTLEY	Scottish
INGLEBY	English (Anglic)	SHOTTON	Scottish
INGLETON	English (Anglic)	WALLISH WALLS	'foreign' (Welsh)
IRESHOPEBURN	Irish	WALWORTH	'foreign' (Welsh)
NORMANBY	Norman, Norse		

PLACE-NAMES WHICH ARE TAUTOLOGICAL

Some of the region's place-names are tautological; the same meaning is given twice. This is usually because an established place-name has no meaning to successive settlers, who speak a different language, and who thus add their own meaningful element.

CONSETT	hilltop hilltop
DALTON LE DALE	farmstead in the valley in the valley
FINDON HILL	heap of wood hill hill
HARLOW HILL	hill of the people hill
HUMBLEDON HILL	bare hill hill
KIRKLEY	hill hill hill
PONTOP	valley valley
PORTGATE	gate gate
WARDEN LAW	watch hill hill

PLACE-NAMES WITH -*TUN*

Old English *tun* was used by the Saxons to denote a general farmstead or small village. It is, of course, the ancestor of modern *town*. The ending -*ton* is very common indeed in North East England, as this list - which is not exhaustive - shows. Other elements in the names may refer to named owners, to position or site of the *tun*, to plants or animals found or reared there, as well as to a number of other descriptive factors. Against each name, I have given the meaning of the other part(s) of the name.

Place-names with -*ington* are listed elsewhere.

ACTON	Acca	ELTON	eels, Aella
ALWINTON	R Alwin	ERRINGTON	Erring Burn
AMERSTON	Amund	ESTON	in the east
BARMPTON	Beornmund	FAWDINGTON	animal fold
BENTON	beans/bentgrass	FELTON	Fygla
BICKERTON	bee-keeper	FENTON	by a fen
BISHOPTON	Bishop	FLOTTERTON	by a 'floating'
BRAFFERTON	wide ford		road
BRANXTON	Brannoc	GLANTON	look-out
BRIERTON	briars	GUNNERTON	Gunnward
BROTTON	brook	HADSTON(E)	Haedda
BRUSSELTON	Beorht	HAGGERSTON	Hagard
CARLTON	peasants	HARRATON	large ford
CHILTON	young man	HARTINGTON	stags' path
CHIRTON	church	HAUGHTON	hill spur
CHOLLERTON	Chollerford	HAVERTON HILL	Haefa, or
CHRISTON BANK	hill		headland
CLAXTON	Clac	HEATON	high
CLIFTON	on a cliff	HILTON	on a hill
COCKERTON	Cocker Beck	HORTON	dirty, muddy
COTHERSTONE	Cuthere	HOUGHTON	hill spur
CRAMLINGTON	cranes' spring	HUTTON	hill spur
DALTON	in a valley	HYLTON	slope, tansy
DENTON	in a valley	ILDERTON	elders
DILSTON	Devil's Water	INGLETON	English
DISSINGTON	by a ditch	IVESTON	Ivo
DUNSTON	Dunn's	KENTON	royal
EGGLESTON	Ecgwulf	KETTON	Ceatta
ELRINGTON	alders		

KIMMERSTON	Cynemaer	SHERATON	Scurfa
LAMBTON	lambs	SHORESTON	Sceot
LANTON	long	SHOTTON	Scots
LINTON	lime-trees or flax	SHOTTON	slope
		SKELTON	shelf-shaped hill
MARTON	lake	STAINTON	paved road
MICKLETON	large	STANNINGTON	paved road
MIDDLETON	in the middle	STANTON	stoney
MILTON	with a mill	STOCKTON	stockaded
MOLESDON	Mol	STRANTON	shore
MONKTON	monks	STURTON	on a Roman road
MORTON	moor	SWAINSTON	Swegen
MURTON	moor	THIRSTON	Thraesfrith
NAFFERTON	Nattfari	THOCKRINGTON	the Unsteady One
NETHERTON	lower	THORNGRAFTON	by a thorn brake
NEWTON	new	THORNTON	thorn trees
NORTON	to the north	THRISLINGTON	Thorstein
NUN STAINTON	nun, stone	THROPTON	at a crossroads
OFFERTON	upper ford	THROSTON	Thori
OUSTON	Ulfkell	WARENTON	Warren Burn
OWTON	Ofa	WELTON	on a spring
PA(W)STON	Palloc	WESTERTON	western
PELTON	Paelli	WALTON	rounded hill
PRESTON	priest	WHORLTON	mill stream
QUARRINGTON	mill	WHORLTON	rounded hill
RAINTON	Regna	WINLATON	Winelac
RICKLETON	Ricela	WHITTON	Hwitta, white
RITTON	on a stream	WILTON	willows
SCREMERSTON	Escrimeur	WITTON	white, or wit
SEATON	by the sea	WOLVISTON	Wulf
SHARPERTON	by a steep hill	WREKENTON	fugitive

THE ROMANS AND PLACE-NAMES

For over a hundred years, this area formed the north-west frontier of the Roman Empire. As such, it was heavily armed and manned, forts and roads were built and - of course - the astonishing Roman Wall was constructed from coast to coast.

Naturally, the Romans named their forts. Although we do not know the names of all their settlements - those at Craster, Whitchester and Outchester, for example - the others _are_ known to us. We even know the meanings of most of them.

ARBEIA was the name of the fort at present-day *SOUTH SHIELDS*. Its meaning is unknown.

BREMENIUM - 'by the roaring stream' - was the fort at present-day *ROCHESTER*.

BROCOLITIA was the fort at what is now *CARRAWBURGH*. Its meaning is unclear; it may denote 'infested with badgers', 'full of pointed rocks' or 'covered with heather'.

CILURNUM was the name given to the fort at present-day *CHESTERS*. Its name seems to be a reference to a 'cauldron' - perhaps the large pool in the river close by.

CONCANIS - 'where the horse people live' - is now *CHESTER LE STREET*. The reference is presumably to the skill of the local people in handling horses.

CORIOSOPITUM or CORSTOPITUM - whose meaning is unknown - is the name given to the fort at present-day *CORBRIDGE*.

HABITANCUM - thought to mean 'land belonging to Habitus' - was at present-day *RISINGHAM*.

LAVATRIS, thought to be a 'latinization' of a native word for 'river-bed', was the fort at present-day *BOWES*.

LONGOVICIUM - thought to mean 'by the pool' or 'place of ship-fighters' - was the fort at what is now *LANCHESTER*.

MORBIUM - meaning unknown - was the fort by the river at present-day *PIERCEBRIDGE*, or perhaps of the fort at *GRETA BRIDGE*.

PONS AELIUS was the name of the fort at what is now *NEWCASTLE UPON TYNE*. The Roman name means 'Aelius' bridge'. *Aelius* was the family name of Hadrian.

SEGEDUNUM was the name of the strategically vital fort at *WALLSEND*; its name is thought to mean 'victory fort' or perhaps 'strong fort'.

VERCOVICIUM - 'the place of good fighters' - was the fort at present-day *HOUSESTEADS*; until comparatively recently it was wrongly called *Borcovicium*.

VINDOBALA is thought to mean 'bright peak'; it is now called *RUDCHESTER*.

VINDOLANDA - the fort at what is now *CHESTERHOLM* - is thought to have meant 'bright moor'.

VINDOMORA - now *EBCHESTER* - probably meant 'bright waters'.

VINOVIA was the fort at present-day *BINCHESTER*; the meaning of the Roman name is unknown.

The list above shows that none of the Latin names survived the Roman withdrawal intact, though the 'shadows' of a few of them seem to have been incorporated into the names given to these sites by Saxon - and sometimes, Viking - settlers who arrived some 100 or so years later. This may have happened at CORBRIDGE (*CORiosopitum*), LANCHESTER (*LONGovicium*) and BINCHESTER *(VINovia)*.

Again, as the list shows, these later Saxon settlers often used Old English *ceastre*, a word borrowed from Latin *castra*, to mean 'the site or ruins of a Roman fort (or other settlement)'. This is why so many of the modern place-names above are variations of *-chester*. For *their* meanings, please see the Dictionary. Hadrian's Wall was, of course, a dramatic enough structure to impress the Saxons who settled near it. Its presence is enshrined in the names below.

BENWELL	inside the Wall
DISSINGTON	by a ditch (of the Wall)
PORTGATE	gap in the Wall
THIRLWALL	gap in the Wall
WALBOTTLE	cottage by the Wall
WALKER	marsh by the wall
WALWICK	dairy farm by the Wall

There are also the settlements of WALL, WALLSEND, WALLTOWN and HEDDON ON THE WALL. The Romans also built roads which were subsequently of such vital importance to Saxon and Viking settlers (whose road-building skills were poor, to say the least) that they were sometimes named. For the meanings of DERE STREET, STANEGATE and WREKENDIKE, see the Dictionary.

SOME PLACE-NAMES WORTH A VISIT

A brief look at the Dictionary shows that many places were named after people or farmsteads that have long since disappeared. Others, though, take their names from geographical features like hills and rivers, or buildings such as churches and Roman forts, which are still very much in evidence today. Visiting these places will help give you a 'feel' for the place-name origin - you will be able to see the name's derivation in front of you.

AUCKLAND *(8m south-west of Durham)*
This name really refers to an area rather than a place; it is the settlements built within its bounds which repay a visit.
BISHOP AUCKLAND is so-named from the palace of the Bishops of Durham, who have had a residence here since the 12th century. Much of what remains is either mediaeval, or of the very early Gothic revival of the 18th century.
ST ANDREW AUCKLAND (SOUTH CHURCH) takes its name from the parish church of St Andrew - the largest in County Durham at 157ft long.
ST HELENS AUCKLAND is named from the parish church of St Helen, built between about 1170 and 1220. This charming little building is easily missed; it stands hidden behind trees by the main A688 road.
BARNARD CASTLE *(in lower Teesdale, 12m west of Darlington)* is, of course, named after the castle built here between 1125 and 1140 by two Bernard Baliols, father and son. It was a large and important building - its enclosure is almost 1,000ft long, and its ruins above steep ravines to the River Tees are still spectacular.
BENWELL *(part of western Newcastle)* is 'inside the Wall' and a valuable relic of it survives here; the only example remaining of masonry-revetted causeway which crossed the vallum of the Wall periodically along its entire length. The ruins of the Roman temple of Antenociticus lie nearby.
BINCHESTER *(1m north of Bishop Auckland)* commemorates the former existence of the Roman fort of Vinovia, the remnants of which can still be seen. Look out for the, Roman central-heating system.
BISHOP MIDDLEHAM *(2m north of Sedgefield)* gained its prefix from the existence here of one of the favourite castles of the Bishops of Durham - two of them died here (in 1283 and 1316). All that remains of the castle are earthworks south of the church.
BISHOPTON *(4m north-west of Stockton)* takes its name from a castle built here in about 1143 for the Bishops of Durham. Impressive earthworks - including a motte standing to 40ft high - are all that remain of the building.
BLACKHALL *(on the coast north of Hartlepool)*
Leave the coast road at Blackhall Rocks to follow a signposted lane to the cliff tops. The rocky foreshore and the 'Black Hall' caves are accessible from here.

CARRAWBURGH *(about 8m north-west of Hexham)*
Like most sites along Hadrian's Wall, this one is windswept and wild. But a short walk will take you to an important remnant of the 'fortification near Carraw' - the Roman fort of *Brocolitia*. It is the temple of Mithras, a cult-god worshipped widely by soldiers of the Roman army.

CASTLE LEVINGTON lies about 2m east of Kirklevington and 2m south of Yarm. The impressive earthwork remains of the Norman castle here comprise a motte over 170ft in diameter standing by the River Leven.

CHESTERHOLM *(about 7m west of Haydon Bridge)* is 'island by a Roman fort'; the fort was *Vindolanda*, and much of it is visible here, including large sections which have been reconstructed to give visitors a better idea of scale and environs than ground-level ruins ever could.

CHESTERS *(near Chollerford)* is simply 'Roman fort'. Here, it was called *Cilurnum*, and much of it has been excavated and is on view. Look out for the bath-house by the river.

CLENNELL *(at Alwinton in upper Coquetdale)*
'The 'clean hill' here is worth climbing for the dramatic cliff-edge earthworks of a prehistoric fort overlooking the River Alwin.

CONSETT *(about 15m south-west of Newcastle)* means 'hilltop', and the commanding site of the town can be better appreciated now that the steelworks which gave it life have vanished.

CORBRIDGE *(3m east of Hexham)*
The first part of this name preserves part of the Roman name of their fort here; *Coriosopitum*. Extensive remains can be seen, including the famous sculptured 'Corbridge Lion'.

DUNSTANBURGH *(on the coast north of Craster)*
The stark and impressive ruins of Dunstanburgh Castle overlie the remains of the prehistoric 'fortification near Dunstan'.

DURHAM is 'hill island', magnificently surmounted since the 11th century by both cathedral and castle.

EBCHESTER *(about 3m north-west of Consett)* marks the site of the first century Roman fort of *Vindomora;* the parish church stands in its south-west corner. The scant remains of the fort, and a small museum, can be visited with the owner's permission.

EGGLESCLIFFE *(on the River Tees opposite Yarm)*
The steep-sided bank which gave Egglescliffe its name is very prominent, and presents a spectacular abutment for the railway viaduct across the Tees and over Yarm's head.

ESTON *(eastern part of Middlesbrough)*
Eston Beacon - or Nab - dominates this part of the Teesside conurbation; the climb to the top can be hard going, but the explorer is rewarded with an ancient and well-preserved hillfort with a rampart still standing to 14ft in places.

GILESGATE *(part of north-eastern Durham City)* is 'the road to the church of St Giles', and the church in question - mostly Norman and mediaeval - offers, as a bonus, spectacular views of Durham Cathedral and Castle,

HAREHAUGH *(about 1m west of Rothbury)*
The ancient British hill-fort which, presumably, gave the 'water-meadow by the old fort' its name is still easily discernible on its promontory above the Coquet.

HARTLEPOOL *(on the coast north-east of Stockton)*
The town took its name as the part of the manor of Hart 'by the sea', and has, in its 1,300 years, undergone many changes. Evidence of its busy history is visible all around; church, town wall, docks, Victorian town hall, eclipsed 20th century gentility and, of course, the sea in its name.

HIGH FORCE *(about 5m west of Middleton-in-Teesdale)* is 'high waterfall' - indeed, the highest in England.

HOLY ISLAND *(off the coast about 9m south of Berwick)* has been a popular destination for visitors for many centuries. The reasons for its name stand all around you here; a ruined priory, an ancient church, a small offshore islet crowned with a cross, and a staked path across the tidal sands which marks the ancient 'Pilgrim's Way'. The island is cut off from the mainland twice daily; be sure to observe safe crossing times.

LANCHESTER *(about 7m north-west of Durham City)*
The remains of the Roman fort of *Longovicium* can be seen from a lay-by on the Satley road, about half a mile outside this pleasant little town.

LANGDON BECK *(at the head of Teesdale)*
The 'long hill' of the name is a striking feature of the stunning Pennine scenery hereabouts.

METAL BRIDGE - there for all to see about 1m east of Spennymoor!

MINDRUM *(about 10m west of Wooler)*
The 'mountain with a ridge' dominates the scenery hereabouts and is available for the stout hearted to climb.

NEWCASTLE UPON TYNE
The 'new castle' which gave the city its name was built by Henry II in 1142-7, and enough of it remains to impress the visitor. See the Keep and the Black Gate, built about 60 years later and now a fascinating museum.

OAKENSHAW *(about 7m west of Durham City)*
The small, rejuvenated mining village is still surrounded by woodland, in the heart of which there is now a wildlife reserve.

PENSHAW *(about 4m west of Sunderland)* may mean 'at the, top of the rocks' - a singularly appropriate name, especially as the 'top' is surmounted by its bizarre Monument. There are fine views from the summit, which, in turn, can be seen from many miles around.

PIERCEBRIDGE *(about 5m west of Darlington)*
As well as the remnants of the fort of *Morbium*, the Roman remains of the 'bridge by the osier willows' are still visible. Amazingly, this bridge remained in use for over 1200 years, until it was replaced by the ancestor of the present bridge across the Tees, further west.

PLENMELLER *(about 3m east of Haltwhistle)*
The 'bare hilltop' is certainly a prominent local feature. The walk to the top is bracing.

ROCHESTER *(about 4m north of Otterburn)*
There are impressive masonry remains of the Roman fort of *Bremenium* here, as well as traces of the trackway of Dere Street (see Dictionary entry), which ran beside it.

ROMALDKIRK *(about 1m south-east of Middleton-in-Teesdale)*
The Church of St Romald, built mostly between the 12th and 14th centuries, still stands at the heart of this typically friendly dales village.

ROSEBERRY TOPPING *(about 3m south-west of Guisborough)*
The distinctive shape of 'Othin's hill' still dominates this part of the region, and the view from the top is worth the climb.

ST JOHN'S CHAPEL *(about 8m west of Stanhope in Weardale)*
The chapel - built in 1752 - which still stands by the small village green is the successor to the original established here in the 14th century, and which gave this Weardale village its name.

SALTBURN BY THE SEA *(on the coast south of Redcar)*
The 'salty burn' still flows into the sea here, crossed by an elegant bridge.

SEAHOUSES *(on the coast opposite the Farne Islands)*
The houses here certainly cluster around the tiny harbour. Ferries to the Farne Islands, about three miles out to sea, leave from here.

SEATON CAREW *(part of southern Hartlepool)* was certainly a 'farmstead by the sea'; at low tide, the long, low, level sands seem to stretch away right across the bay to Redcar.

STANGHOW *(about 5m south-east of Middlesbrough)*
No sign of the *stang* - the pole - but the *how* ('hill') affords views all around this area of East Cleveland.

TOW LAW *(about 12m west of Durham City)* occupies one of the most exposed sites for a settlement of this size in the entire area and is, indeed, an ideal 'look-out hill'. The best views are probably from the main road entering the town to the south-west.

WARDEN LAW *(1m east of Houghton-le-Spring)* certainly deserves its name - 'the watch-hill'. There are extensive views from here, and the small windfarm adds an arguable grandeur to the site.

See the separate Digest entry for sites associated with Hadrian's Wall.

NAMES OF LOST PLACES

We have long been used to the inexorable growth of places; over the centuries, small farms got bigger and some of them became hamlets. In turn, some of these developed into villages and towns.

Some settlements, though, have gone in the opposite direction. The English countryside is dotted with the sites of farms, hamlets and even quite substantial villages whose inhabitants deserted them, and which have been abandoned to decay, to the plough and to nature. Archaeologists call thein 'DMVs' - deserted mediaeval villages.

There are many reasons why settlements were abandoned like this. In the mid-14th century, for example, the Black Death wiped out up to 70% of England's population, including, of course, whole villages.

North East England - and especially County Durham - possesses an unusually large number of places which have, over the centuries, shrunk to a shadow of their mediaeval selves, or have disappeared altogether, leaving only a few indentations in the ground, or no trace at all.

For the curious explorer, all of these sites are marked on standard Ordnance Survey maps, though you should note that access can sometimes be difficult.

ABBERWICK
In north Northumberland, and just a few yards west of the more recent village of Abberwick which replaced it.
ANCROFT
In the heart of the central Northumberland countryside, and close to the more recent village of the same name.
BELSAY
The ancient village lay between the castle and the Hall. It was swept away in the mid-19th century when Sir Charles Monck Middleton designed and built the 'new' Belsay we see today.
ESP GREEN (probably Old English 'aspen green')
About 1.5m north-west of Lanchester. Though now just a farmhouse, there was once a substantial farming settlement here, complete with chapel. This village itself was built over the remains of a Roman/Ancient British hamlet. Earthworks can still be seen.

GARMONDSWAY
The earthworks which mark the site of this abandoned village are still clearly visible and well-preserved near Trimdon.

COLD HESLEDON
The ancient village lay between the present-day East and West Farms, about 3m north of Easington (County Durham). It had already been abandoned when a new 19th century village grew up around the colliery and waterworks. This village, too, has disappeared.

LANGETON
Only a few undulations in the ground mark the site of Langeton. They lie a few yards west of the village of Lanton, which replaced it, in the heart of Northumberland.

LUDWORTH
The present village is a creation of 19th century colliery development and lies a little east of the mediaeval Ludworth, which was centred around Ludworth Tower, only a fragment of which survives. The ancient village is thought to have been abandoned by 1450. Earthworks, including those of an ancient watermill, can still be seen, about 6m east of Durham City.

EAST MATFEN
The village lay a few yards south-west of modern Matfen; its remnants can he traced easily in the earth at the site.

OXEN LE FIELDS
Only a solitary farm reminds us of this village, which has otherwise completely disappeared, a few miles south-east of Darlington.

PITTINGTON HALLGARTH
A very much reduced version of its mediaeval predecessor, about 5m north-east of Durham City; earthworks of the Prior's Manor House, and other ancient houses, can he seen just north of the churchyard.

SADBERGE
In mediaeval times, Sadberge was an important manor and the village was really a small town by the standards of the time. The small, rather pretty, village we see today reveals almost nothing of its history. It lies by the A66 a few miles east of Darlington.

SEAHAM
The village of Old Seaham, on the coast south of Sunderland, has completely disappeared. It lay all around the ancient church (which still stands) and between it and nearby Seaham Hall.

SHOTTON
About 2m west of Cockfield. Only scant earthworks remain.

SNOTTERTON (which may be Old English 'Snotra's farmstead')
West of Staindrop. Nothing at all remains of the village.

STAINSBY

The remains of the original, ancient village of Stainsby now mostly lie under the A19 road south of Teesside. You can see traces of them just a few yards east of the present suburban settlement of Stainsby.

THORNLEY (near Wheatley Hill)

Modern Thornley is a 19th century mining village; ancient Thornley lay about 1m south, around Thornley Hall, which still exists. Substantial earthworks are still visible; they include the village's main street, or 'hollow way', now defined as an ash-tree avenue.

TOWN KELLOE

About 3m east of Coxhoe, this is probably County Durham's most easily discernible deserted village. Remnants of two ancient village rows, as well as of other demolished buildings, are clearly visible around Kelloe Hall here.

ULNABY

Indeterminate bumps in the ground near the Hall are all that remain of ancient Ulnaby, about 5m west of Darlington.

WALWORTH

A large mediaeval village - perhaps even a small, failed borough - lay north of the present Hall here, about 5m west of Darlington. At least three rows of houses faced a small green, on which the present North Farm stands; the remains of a chapel are built into its walls. Two further rows of houses lay a little to the north-east.

OLD WINGATE

Nothing except a farm remains of this village, which lay about 1m south of Wheatley Hill.

YODEN (probably a version of *Horden* - see Dictionary)

Uneven bumps in the ground are all that remain of this long-abandoned village, now on the north-eastern edge of Peterlee (at Eden Hill).

PLACE-NAMES WHICH FEATURE LOCAL VARIATION

Local people sometimes ensure that place-names are not what they seem. They may use unexpected or unusual pronunciations; they may divide the settlement into 'unofficial' parts; they may even use a different name altogether.

All of the names below have local variations of one sort or another. The length of the list is testament to enduring local folk-memory.

ALNMOUTH is pronounced *alnmth*.
ALNWICK is pronounced *anick*.
BLACKHALL is divided into *Colliery* and *Rocks* by local people.
BOLAM is pronounced *bow-lm*.
BOULMER is pronounced *boome*r.
BOURNMOOR The first element is pronounced *burn*.
BROOM is called *Broompark* by local people.
BUDLE is pronounced *byoodl*.
BYSHOTTLES Found on maps, this old name is not used at all.
CHESTER LE STREET is almost always referred to simply as *Chester*; its citizens are *Cestrians*.
CORNSAY The original hilltop settlement is known locally as *Old Cornsay*.
DENWICK is pronounced *dennick*.
EARLE is pronounced *yerl*.
EASINGTON is always divided into *Colliery* and *Village*.
FINCHALE is pronounced *finkle*.
HOUGHALL - part of Durham City - is pronounced *hoffl*.
HULAM is pronounced *hugh-lm*.
HULNE is pronounced *hool*, rhyming with 'school'.
KEPIER is pronounced *keepyer*,
KILLHOPE is *killup*.
KININVIE has stress on the last syllable; *kin-in-VEE*.
KYO is *k-eye-o*.
MORWICK is pronounced *morick*.
NUNWICK is pronounced *nunnick*.
OUSTON is *oostn*.
PASTON is pronounced as it is often spelt; *Pawston*.
PELAW is *pee-law*.
PONTELAND is pronounced with stress on the second syllable; *PontEland*.
ROOKHOPE is *roo-kup*.
ROWLEY rhymes with *Cowley*.
SACRISTON is sometimes still called *Seggison* or *Seggiston* by some local people.

ST ANDREW AUCKLAND is almost always referred to as *South Church*.

SHERBURN is always divided into *Village*, *Hill* and *Hospital*.

STANHOPE is *stan-up*.

TANTOBIE has stress on the second syllable: *tant-O-bie*.

THORPE is usually called *Little Thorpe* by local people.

TOW LAW The first word rhymes with *cow*.

TRIMDON STATION is almost always called *Deaf Hill*.

ULGHAM is pronounced *uffm*.

USHAW is pronounced *Usher*, and is referred to as *Ushaw Moor* by local people.

WALWICK is pronounced *wolick*.

WINGATE is pronounced *wingut*.

WITTON GILBERT The second word is pronounced *Jilbert*.

In Northumberland, many local people pronounce place-names in that county ending with *-ingham* with a 'soft' *g*; that is, as *-injm*. For indeterminate reasons, this does not apply to *Chillingham*.

Ponteland, Northumberland

ODD AND UNUSUAL NAMES

The place-names below have unusual characteristics of one kind or another. The list is only a selection; for many people, local place-names have a unique interest of their own.

ANNFIELD PLAIN is one of the region's few place-names (another is *Metal Bridge*) to mention an industrial structure - in this case, an inclined plane for colliery tubs.

AYDON
Two places with the same name - but each with a different meaning. This phenomenon is, in fact, not uncommon, and place-name enthusiasts should therefore beware!

BALDERSDALE
A possible example of what place-name people call 'back-formation'; it works like this. Most river-valleys take their names from the rivers that flow through them. Thus, *Teesdale* is 'valley of the River Tees' and *Allendale* is 'valley of the River Allen'. At *Baldersdale*, though, it is thought that the river takes its name from the valley. So *Balder* is 'river that flows through Baldersdale'. *Baldersdale* itself means 'valley belonging to Baldhere'. Other examples of this topsy-turvy process are included below.

BLANCHLAND is a peculiarly graceful and understandably French-sounding name for its situation in deepest rural northern England.

BLAYDON is known the world over as the site of the Races in the song which has become the unofficial Geordie 'national anthem'.

BRANCEPETH, like many place-names, has given rise to a folk-explanation; that it was the 'brawn's path' used by the fearsome Brawn of Brancepeth, which was eventually killed by Hodge of Ferry.

BUTTERBY is mentioned in an old local saying; 'to go to church at Butterby' is not to go to church at all - there is no church there!

CARGO FLEET is a name as old as most in this book. Yet an accident of geography and history has placed it in the heart of Teesside's docks, where most people therefore think of it as a modern, industrial name.

CARLIN HOW
The hill where witches - or at least extremely ugly old women - once gathered is still, of course, there to climb!

CASTLE EDEN is known all over England; the brewery here named a very popular beer after the village.

COLD HESLEDON, like *Wingate*, mentions how inclement the local weather could be - and still is.

COQUET

Another example of back-formation - see *Baldersdale*, above. The River Coquet takes its name from *Coquetdale* - 'valley of the wild bird wood' - rather than the normal way round.

CULLERCOATS is one of those odd names that seems to mean something in modern English!

EGGLESCLIFFE is a rare example of Victorian flight of fancy; the railway company changed it to *Eaglescliffe*, presumably to make it sound more romantically 'dramatic'.

ESH WINNING is, as far as I can tell, the only place in England to use the word *winning* in its name.

FAREWELL HALL is just a pleasingly eccentric name whose precise meaning may only be guessed at.

FLEMINGFIELD, like *Shotton*, *Shotley*, *Walworth*, *Ireshopeburn*, and *Normanby,* is proof that the racial mix was extensive even 1,500 years ago. Here we have a Belgian, a Scot, a Welshman, an Irishman and a Norman.

FLOTTERTON

Some place-names mention constructions or contraptions of various kinds built for various purposes. In this name, there is a reference to a 'floating road'; perhaps it was a causeway laid on rushes and rafts in some way. Certainly, whatever was at the other end must have been valuable to the Anglo-Saxon settlers who built it. See also *KEPIER, WYLAM* and *YARM*, amongst others.

GAUNLESS

We can only guess at why our ancestors chose to brand this innocent little river as 'useless'!

GUIDE POST

The post in question must have been particularly impressive to bestow a name to the settlement which developed around it and the crossroads it overlooked.

HARLE

A rare and revealing reference to heathenism, which must have been practised illicitly long after Christianity had become the official religion of the Saxons. *HARROWGATE, WOOPERTON* and perhaps *GATESHEAD* may also give the game away.

HEXHAM

A diverting snippet of Saxon social history is preserved in this name - see the Dictionary entry. One of those place-names with a story to tell.

INGLEBY

Another name - like *Flemingfield* above - that shows the racial mix of the region in the years before the Norman Conquest. An Angle, of the race which gave its name to *England*, lived here, and at *Ingleton*.

INKERMAN, like *Toronto*, *Quebec* and the much-depleted colliery village of *Heights of Alma*, has adopted the name of a British colonial conquest overseas - although it is not always clear why.

JARROW, like *Hexham* above, enshrines a rare reference to Anglo-Saxon social history and - in this case - to what may have been economic migration. The name commemorates the tribe of 'fen-people' who must have moved here from the East Midlands. A similar story may well be told by *LINDISFARNE*, to which a North Lincolnshire tribe may have migrated.

KEPIER

The name of this small, riverside settlement outside Durham preserves a rare reference to a man-made contraption, in this case constructed by the Saxons to catch fish. See *WYLAM*, *YARM* and *FLOTTERTON*, too.

LESBURY

Several place-names in this book commemorate the occupations of the settlers; look in the Digest. But here, the settler's job is concealed behind the dialect word 'leech', used - perhaps suspiciously - by the Saxons to indicate a 'doctor'!

LOFTUS - 'house with an upper storey' - gives an accidental insight into how rare such houses ordinarily must have been when the existence of one of them is remarked in this way.

MORPETH

Most of the places in this book straightforwardly acquired their names from local features like rivers, hills, moors, fields, plants and animals; or from the names of the folk who settled them. *Morpeth* is a great rarity; it seems to commemorate an historical event - a murder. We will, of course, never know the circumstances of this occurrence, but it must have been particularly brutal and bloody for the name to have stuck so firmly to the settlement. See also *SOCKBURN*, below.

NEWCASTLE UPON TYNE is a rare example of a place that has had three different and unrelated names in its history. The Romans called it *Pons Aelius*, 'Hadrian's bridge', the Saxons called it *Monkchester*, 'Roman fort of the monks', and we call it 'new castle'.

PENNINES is a rare example of a deliberately-invented 'antique-sounding' name. The name is brilliant - many people believe it to be very ancient indeed!

PETERLEE is probably the only place in England to adopt a person's name as its own.

RATCHWOOD would be 'wretch's wood' in Modern English. The curious may be keen to know why this wood was used so frequently by outlaws that it came to be named after them. We will have to contain their curiosity; we will never know. For other unsavoury types, see *Scrainwood*, *Wrekendike* and *Wreigh Burn/Wreighill*.

SETTLING STONES appears to be a corruption of 'saddling stones', the boulders or large rocks which riders would use to help them remount their horses after the steep climb up Grindon Hill; they would have dismounted at the bottom.

SOCKBURN seems to be in the same league as *Morpeth*, above. It commemorates an historical event - in this case, some sort of judicial enquiry or court, about which we know no more.

SHINCLIFFE contains a rare reference to the spirit world.

SHITLINGTON and SHITTLEHOPE have a unique point of interest; they are lucky to have survived at all. With the strength of Victorian prudery and 'delicacy', many place-names with elements like this were ruthlessly altered to make them less offensive to the easily-shocked. Fearlessly, no changes were made to these two though.

SHOTTON

Like *Walworth*, *Ingleby* and some others, a name to remind us of the tribal, racial mix of the region, even in 'the Dark Ages'. There were Scots here - and at *SHOTLEY*.

SMALES BURN

A degree of 'back-formation' has occurred with this name. See the Dictionary entry and *Baldersdale*, above.

SPITAL TONGUES, SPITTAL and SPITTLE

Apart from their unfortunate sound-link to Modern English, these colourful names remind us of the existence of hostels and hospitals - 'spittles' - in pre-Conquest Britain. They were as often for the benefit of cold, wet and tired travellers as they were for the local sick.

THORPE THEWLES frustratingly keeps its secret; what exactly did the villagers do to earn the nickname 'immoral'?

UNTHANK may prove that our Saxon forebears also had trouble with squatters; it seems to mean 'without permission'!

WANSBECK

This river-name may incorporate a degree of 'back-formation'; it appears to be named after a bridge that crossed it. See the Dictionary entries for this and COQUET, also named by back-formation. (For 'back-formation', see *Baldersdale*, above.)

AND FINALLY.....

North East England is the proud possessor of some of the country's oddest place-names. All of these have been listed elsewhere, but grouped together they make quite a list!

AMBLE, BAGRAW, BEARPARK, BLACK MIDDENS, BLANCHLAND, BUDLE, BYSHOTTLES, CALIFORNIA, CAMBO, CAMBOIS, CARGO FLEET, CHIPCHASE. CO-OPERATIVE VILLAS, CRONKLEY, CUSHAT LAW, DEAF HILL, DELVES, DEVIL'S WATER, DIRT POT, DRAGONVILLE, DUDDO, ETAL, FAREWELL HALL, FATFIELD, GUYZANCE, HAZON, HELM, HETT, HOLE, HOPPYLAND, INKERMAN, KYO, LINTZ, MERRYBENT, METAL BRIDGE, NEW YORK, NO PLACE, OGLE, PHILADELPHIA, PITY ME, QUAKINGHOUSES, QUEBEC, RYLE, SLAGGYFORD, SNITTER, SPITAL TONGUES, SPITTLE, TIPTOE, TORONTO, VIGO, WHAM, WIDE OPEN and WITHERWACK.

Other books from G P Electronic Services

Tyneside: Past and Present

Over 100 photographs of Tyneside as it used to be alongside views of the present day. Intriguing facts and information about each photograph along with a descriptive journey around Tyneside which shows the reader the views in the order as they appear in the book.

Price: £6.95   ISBN 0 9522480 0 X

Newcastle: Then and Now

Earlier books by Geoff Phillips have mainly featured photographs of Newcastle upon Tyne and Tyneside as it was in the late 1800's and early 1900's. This book compares Newcastle upon Tyne today with a time that many people will remember; the 1950's and 1960's. As in earlier books, there are nearly always links between the old and new photographs. Sometimes these links are very hard to find which adds to the enjoyment of the book.

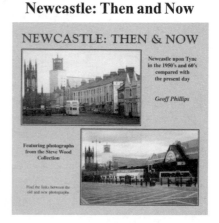

Price: £6.95   ISBN 0 9522480 5 0

Memories of Tyne Tees Television

The book is mainly about the early years of TTT (1959 to mid sixties) and includes many intriguing stories about the programmes and the people and features interviews with Mike Neville, Bill Steel, David Hamilton and many more personalities.

Price: £9.95   ISBN 0 9522480 6 9
All Prices include postage & packing

All books are obtainable where you bought this book, or by mail order from
G P Electronic Services, 87 Willowtree Avenue, Durham City DH1 1DZ.   Tel 0191 384 9707

Other books from G P Electronic Services

Newcastle: Past & Present - Millennium Edition
Geoff Phillips

Views of Newcastle upon Tyne in the late 19th century and early 20th century along with new photographs taken from the same vantage points

Price: £9.95 ISBN 0 9522480 7 7

If, as we say, "one picture is worth a thousand words", then any single one of the photographs of Newcastle from the book 'Newcastle: Past & Present' can inspire at least a thousand rich and telling words. But, what if we then couple the picture with another one taken at the same place 65 years on, and then link that one with a third taken a further 30 years later? Well, we get much more than a few thousand words - instead we get a precious glimpse into the turning world of time and change, which gives each chosen location its own special mystery and unique sense of place.

David Lovie - Heritage Officer, Grainger Town Project

All books are obtainable where you bought this book, or by mail order from
G P Electronic Services, 87 Willowtree Ave, Durham City DH1 1DZ.